ALSO BY MICHELENE WANDOR

Shibboleths and Ploughshares

Shibboleth: catchword, esp. Old-fashioned and generally abandoned doctrine or formula of a party or sect (Heb., ear of corn).

Ploughshares: implement for cutting furrows in soil and turning it in.

(The Concise Oxford Dictionary)

Shibboleths and Ploughshares

Music

emotion   meaning   performance

Michelene Wandor

prima la musica!

Prima la musica!

First published in Great Britain in 2023

Shibboleths and Ploughshares
Michelene Wandor © 2023

michelenewandor.co.uk

Printed and bound by imprintdigital.com
Prima la Musica website: www.primalamusica.com

Cataloguing in Publication Data
is available from the British Library
ISBN: 978-1-399965-29-3

CONTENTS

PREFACE

I AM TEN. Someone arrives in the village with a handful of descant recorders for the children. I am ill, and miss the handout. There's a spare recorder, and one of the other children shows me where to put my fingers for G, and where the note is on the treble clef. I teach myself to read music by playing folk songs from a book, recognising the tunes and seeing where the notes are on the page. I am a good student; a fast learner. I love it.

In London, as a teenager, listening to 'Woman's Hour' on the Home Service (later Radio 4), and the signature tune fires me. I write to the BBC, and they tell me it is 'Badinerie' from Bach's Orchestral Suite number 2, in b minor. I find a small music shop in Walthamstow and buy the pocket score. I have never heard of Bach. I love the tune. I play it.

I buy another Bach pocket score: the Italian Concerto. I am in the sixth form at Chingford County High School. Mr Davies, the Welsh music master, is impressed with my facility on the descant. To the suppressed amusement of fellow students, I play the top line of the first movement of the Italian Concerto at the end of year concert. Mr Davies accompanies me at the piano. Before I leave school, he suggests I should play a 'proper' instrument. I buy a clarinet, like the sound, and can play fast. I know nothing about music, nothing about keys, but I can read the notes and play.

At Newnham College, Cambridge, reading English, I meet a friend on the first day. She plays the clarinet. We play duets, we join an outdoor brass band, and she tells me about her nice teacher. I have my first music lessons. One day my clarinet squeaks, the nice teacher laughs, and that's it for me and the clarinet.

From then on I play my descant very fast, alone in my room. I have acquired a gramophone, and have two records; the Brandenburg Concertos (I like this Bach music a lot) and another friend gives me a record of someone called Julian Bream, playing Dowland. I'm not sure whether I like that or not.

I go to nine am lectures on medieval poetry, given by John Stevens. He sings strange music in a light, sweet, unselfconscious voice. I think it quaint, but I am more into learning to jive to Elvis Presley and the Everly Brothers.

In 1962, I graduate from Cambridge. That year, Thurston Dart became Chair of Music at Cambridge. Raymond Leppard was Director of Music at Trinity College. Christopher Hogwood arrived at Pembroke College in 1960, followed by David Munrow in 1961. My American husband-to-be was at Pembroke College that year, so I got to know the place rather well. Not once did I hear a peep out of a recorder, or a boom out of a bassoon, both (I later learn) played by Munrow. So near and yet so far. Courtesy of my boyfriend, I acquire aural knowledge of jazz: Coltrane, Sonny Rollins, Miles Davis, Ella Fitzgerald, Bill Evans. My recorder remains closeted.

It is 1976/7. I take my younger son to a Saturday Young Music Makers' guitar class, in London's Gospel Oak. They have 'classes' for parents who bring their musical prodigy offspring for lessons. I join a recorder group (my descant, with German F fingering), run by Alan Lumsden, who suggests I should also play the treble. He sells me the double album of David Munrow's *The Art of the Recorder*. This is my introduction to 'early music'.

I go to Morley College recorder consort evening classes. Morley College was part of the Nineteenth-Century Adult Education Movement, which organised classes for 'working people'. Morley originated in a building near Waterloo, which later became the Old Vic Theatre. Gustav Holst was Director of Music, 1907-1924, followed later by Michael Tippett, 1940-1951.

I join one of Theo Wyatt's recorder consorts, and he encourages me to play the whole family of recorders. From here on it is really fast forward. Theo organises weekend and week-long recorder courses, and on these I discover repertoire. On a North London Saturday recorder group-playing afternoon, I come across Philip Thorby, who teaches recorder at Trinity College of Music, in London.

He conducts, coaxes, encourages, wittily castigates. Out of a motley (let's be honest) out-of-tune group, he produces a relatively harmonious finale. There was sound, there was aesthetic, though I would not then have identified it as such. I begin going to early music concerts, and hear Philip Thorby's group, Musica Antiqua of London, whose Renaissance repertoire, tiny pieces of music, skeined to create musical paragraphs, brings a new sound, the viola da gamba.

I have always earned my living as a professional writer, part of it as an arts reviewer. Between 1988 and 1991 I reviewed concerts and CDs of Renaissance and Baroque music (for 'Early Music News', 'Time Out' and 'The Guardian'), steering clear of technical comments (I knew nothing about music's systems), testing language to express the impressions, impact, presentation, created by the performances. Using verbal language (words) to describe/review the non-verbal arts (especially painting and music) was (and is) not easy.

Alongside the reviewing, a desire emerges to know more about what is happening when playing consort music. I have considerable experience of dramatic performance – radio, theatre, television. I know what happens there; but what is the music 'doing', if anything? Is the music about emotion or sound, or something else? Does it matter? The *feel* and sound of playing is crucial. I want consort playing to sound 'better', to have a feeling of ensemble, so that what we produce is complete and satisfying.

Retrospectively, I had a professional approach to being an

amateur; I was seeking an aesthetic. This was not popular in amateur circles, where the saying went, 'as long as you enjoy it, that's the main thing'. However, I did not enjoy out-of-tune playing, I did not enjoy ragged ensemble. With or without an audience, playing music was, and is, a performance. But a performance of what? And how? And was there emotion in it?

I approached Philip Thorby for recorder lessons. He agreed, and I imagine they were as taxing for him (from a different perspective) as they were for me. I played solo recorder music for the first time. It was an ear-opener. The core of the teaching/learning process was a combination of technique (articulation) and shaping, phrasing – call it expression. I tried to play as instructed. I had a vague sense that playing the music related to melodic and harmonic shapes, but I did not 'know' what they were. I had had no music lessons, never done scales, knew nothing about keys or harmony. I could read and play, whatever that meant.

Was music a language, with a grammar? It certainly was a system. And, just as people can learn to speak and read without knowing about grammar, could one read and play music without knowing the system? I wanted to play better, and know more about what I was doing.

Trinity College of Music accepted me for a one-year postgraduate course as a mature student, at the end of the 1980s, in the tiny Department of Renaissance and Baroque Music: individual lessons (recorder and viol) and consort coaching. One year extended into the four-year Performer's course, and finally, to the MMus.

During these years, I was writing as much as ever. This is important, not just because it enabled me to pay college fees and buy instruments, but because I was engaging with two art forms and modes; one utterly verbal in its essence, the other utterly non-verbal in its essence. The language in lessons and consort coaching was directed, focussed, 'practical', performative, productive. It was not conceptually analytical; it was not evaluative or contextual. That was not a problem, but it raised questions I wanted to think and write about.

The MMus was a way to continue improving my playing, and to find a way to get language to take music on board. My final dissertation traced, analysed and evaluated the three tenets of the early music movement: authenticity, interpretation and intention. I also wrote essays independently on music and aesthetics, emotion, meaning and performance, and on idiomatic music.

Was music a language, or like a language? Did it have a grammar, beyond the merely technical, systems-based? What was it 'about', what was it 'doing', what did it mean, if anything? Was it about sound or emotion, or something else? What relationship did all these questions have to performance? Does it matter?

I am not the only person to think that these questions have not been definitively answered. Two recent books: *Rethinking Hanslick*[1] and *Music and Aesthetic Reality*[2] reassess Eduard Hanslick, the nineteenth-century writer on aesthetics. His investigation of the relationship between music, meaning, emotion and expression, still resonates.

This book reworks my MMus dissertation, together with my essays and new material. In the process, it branches out into the broader musicological issues of aesthetics, meaning, emotion, idiomatic music and the conditions of performance, leading into discussions of early music with its three central tenets. Some of the ideas may be controversial, but that is always a good thing!

As well as contributing to academic discussion, I hope the book will open up the ideas to students – school, conservatoire, college,

---

1 *Rethinking Hanslick: Music, Formalism and Expression*, ed. Nicole Grimes, Soibhan Donovan and Wlfgang Marx (Boydell and Brewer, 2015)
2 *Music and Aesthetic: Reality Formalism and the Limits of Description*, by Nick Zangwill (Routledge, 2015)

university, music teachers, as well as professional and amateur musicians – even audiences.

INTRODUCTION

Music, Emotion, Meaning and Performance

THE SUBTITLE OF THIS hybrid book merits some deconstruction. My MMus dissertation (part of Chapter Seven) briefly historicised the 'early music revival', with its scholarly excavation and performance of neglected music. Three tenets emerged from this largely twentieth-century process. Authenticity encompassed both the 'hardware' of the reconstruction of instruments modelled on their historic precedents, and the 'software' of making the music available to today's world. Interpretation abutted onto the editing/publication of this revived music, and its performance. Finally, Intention aimed to fold together the relationship between present and past, by claiming a symbiotic link between composers and performers. This pre-classical music created discrete spaces, and its ideas and approaches have influenced what is now called 'historically informed performance', which can be applied to music from any time.

Behind these categories hovers the long-standing issue of hermeneutics and aesthetics; meaning and the significance of the art form. Theories and methodologies of interpretation have tried to tackle some of these questions: what is music, what is it 'about'? If it has content, of what does this consist? What does music 'do', and, above all, what does/may it 'mean'?

In both my playing and writing, these questions came up in a variety of ways, and were informed by the radical cultural thought of the 1970s and 1980s. This addressed the arts in their social contexts, in relation to gender and its political impact. Similar discussions influenced the New Musicology, spurred by an article in 1980: 'How We Got into Analysis, and How to Get Out'.[3] Joseph Kerman called for 'a new breadth and flexibility in academic music criticism [musicology]'.

A series of books helped to develop the New Musicology. *Man and Music* (in the US with the more enlightened *Music and Society)* aimed to 'present music in a broad context of socio-political, economic, intellectual and religious life'.[4] Iain Fenlon pointed out that, while compositional techniques, forms and styles had their own histories, the books aimed to relate music to:

> ... *changes in the function of music itself, which are in turn responses to changes in the structures and needs of society ... religious change, the impact of printing and the growth in influence of the bourgeoisie, all of which are intimately and inextricably related ...* [5]

Further examples can be seen in *Musical Instruments and their Symbolism in Western Art* which pioneered musical iconology.[6] Winternitz analysed the symbolic function of pictorial structure in delineating the social status of musicians (high or low), and the religious, erotic and political meanings associated with various instruments. For example, wind instruments were supposedly thought to convey sexual symbolism. Sounds were thought to have meanings in themselves. This approach is continued in *Music and Image*[7] which focuses on eighteenth-century painting and English domestic music-making. Other musicologists, such as Susan McClary, in *Feminine Endings*[8] have produced valuable insights into the place (often the non-place) of

---

3   Kerman, Joseph, *Write it all Down: Essays on Music* (University of California Press, 1994)
4   Blurb to *The Renaissance*, ed. Iain Fenlon (Prentice Hall, 1989)
5   Ibid
6   Winternitz, Emanuel (Yale University Press, 1979)
7   Leppert, Richard (CUP, 1993)
8   University of Minnesota Press, 1991

women in musical history, opening up the question of the relationship between music and gender.

Underneath these material investigations, more conceptual/theoretical questions remain, with the most pertinent point of departure in Eduard Hanslick's 1854 book, *The Beautiful in Music*.[9] Hanslick set out the broad musicological issues of aesthetics, meaning, emotion and performance, which still track our discussions today. In his effort to reconcile early nineteenth-century Romantic notions with developing scientific ways of thinking, Hanslick emerges as remarkably 'modern' in part of his clearly materialist approach to music. See later for caveats in other parts of his approach.)

Shibboleths and Ploughshares also begins with Hanslick. Chapter 1, **History, Music and Aesthetics,** presents the framework of his arguments (and their limitations), followed by ways in which early twentieth-century musicologists have continued, or contested his ideas on aesthetics. Chapter 2, **Music, Emotion and Meaning,** explores ways of thinking about these matters. In both chapters, my distillations include illustrative quotations from the writers, to give a flavour of their voices, vocabularies and points of view. While some accounts are inevitably schematic, I hope that these 'tasters' will lay out lines of discussion, and encourage readers to follow up the writers in more detail.

Chapter 3, **Music into Performance,** presents interviews with conservatoire teachers and performers (including Sir Roger Norrington) to get a sense of how they think and communicate matters of expression, meaning and emotion in their work with students and professional musicians. Chapter 4, **The Conditions of Performance,** analyses four different productions of Bach's *St Matthew Passion*, in different venues and under different circumstances, to offer an interpretation of the ways in which meanings are created by the contexts and presentation of

---

9   Translated by Gustav Cohen (Novello, 1891)

performance itself, and how these relate to/conflict with any 'messages' in the verbal content of the work.

Chapter 5, **Idiomatic Music 1,** heralds the exciting way in which the excavation of pre-nineteenth-century music has prompted some important rethinking of musical assumptions. With illustrations, the flexibility in notation and instrumentation (and thence into 'interpretation') overturns notions of musical determinism, showing, in particular, the limitations of 'intention'. Chapter 6, **Idiomatic Music 2: Women and the High Viol** teases the deconstruction of idiomatic music via the insights of feminist/ gender-based analysis to show how, for a brief historical moment, the high viol was primarily (though not completely) associated with women. The chapter also argues that unthinking, and still prejudiced, assumptions about gender permeate the vocabulary of musical analysis.

Chapter 7, **The Early Music Revival: authenticity, interpretation, invention**, returns full-blown to early music. Adding to the insights of the New Musicology, the chapter uncovers George Bernard Shaw's contribution to the revival, in his musical criticism, as well as showing how the early music revival was not a hermetic development. Rather, it was inextricably interwoven with early twentieth-century ideas about religion and literature. The landmark offerings of Dolmetsch, Dart and Donington are charted; from these, the three key concepts of authenticity, interpretation and intention are examined, to return to one of the central ideas of this book: that meaning and emotion are associative and contextual (*pace* Hanslick!). The apple may not fall far from the tree, but its journey is complex and multi-faceted, and is far from ended.

Finally, the Preface and Codas offer something of an autobiographical framing, to explain my relationship with early music, and to bring my work as a writer to the service of experimenting with what I think/hope were some original combinations of words and early music.

This book distils a wide range of ideas, historical moments and concepts (*multum in parvo*). I hope it will help to demonstrate that the understanding of an art form must entail a sense of hybridity. This may challenge some experts, while opening up new ways of thinking about music to others for the first time.

I contend that the questions Hanslick asked still need to be asked, discussed and argued over. Is music a language, or like a language? Is it just a set of technical/mathematical sonic systems? Does it have grammar/s? What is it about? What is it 'doing'? What does it mean, if anything? What is the relationship between emotion and music, if anything? Does any of this matter?

These questions are only the beginning.

PART ONE

CHAPTER ONE

History, Music and Aesthetics

Introduction

> *We are born into society, we are born into history. No moment comes when we are offered a ticket of admission with the option to reject it.*[10]

E. H. Carr argues that all histories are, in some form, products of the times in which they are thought and written. He counters a view of history in which ideas and events are seen merely as the products of Great Men (*sic*). We have no choice about the world we are born into, or the ideas about it which greet us. However, we inevitably interact with our worlds, and may or may not argue with what we find:

> *... history consists essentially in seeing the past through the eyes of the present and in the light of its problems.*[11]

Carr points out that in each historical phase, particular world views hold sway. The Greeks had:

> *... visions of a return to a golden age of the past – a critical view which assimilated the processes of history to the processes of nature ... It was the Jews, and after them the Christians, who introduced an entirely new element by postulating a goal towards which the historical process is moving – the teleological view of history ... This was the medieval view of history. The Renaissance restored the*

---

10   Carr, E. H., *What is History?* (Pelican, 1972)
11   Ibid, p21

classical view of an anthropocentric world and of the primacy of reason... History became progress towards the goal or the perfection of man's (sic) estate on earth ... The cult of progress reached its climax at the moment when British prosperity, power and self-confidence were at their height ... in the full flood of Victorian optimism ...[12]

This view of history derives from a belief that the 'productive forces' in society shape and help to determine what we call ideas and imagination, and generate what we call 'art'. Indeed, the concept of art, as we use it today, only came into being in the modern age:

Aristotelian poetics, that is, the teaching of poeisis, was a theory of making and producing. The notion of creating was foreign to ancient and medieval art criticism.[13]

Carr's view is not crude, schematic or reductivist. It allows for each art form to have its own particular history, while acknowledging that it has an active, and interactive, relationship with its surrounding society. This is relevant in any discussion of aspects of aesthetic thought which attempt to understand what music 'is', and what it may 'mean'.

Carl Dalhaus points out that the development of aesthetics as an intellectual discipline is relatively recent. Alexander Baumgarten popularised the term in his book, *Aesthetica*, published in 1750. Before that, two views of music had held sway:

The idea that music's goal was to represent and arouse affections is a commonplace, rooted as deeply in history as the opposing thesis that music is sounding mathematics.[14]

Baumgarten's 'theory of perception' countered the primacy of eighteenth-century logic and reason. He 'aimed at justifying the

---

12   Ibid, pp. 110-112
13   Dalhaus, Carl, *Esthetics of Music*, trans. William Austin (CUP, 1990, p2)
14   Ibid, p17

emancipation of sensuous perception, claiming that such perceptions were a kind of knowledge in themselves.[15] The dialogue between reason and emotion had other consequences in the 18th century. As Dalhaus asserts, there was a preoccupation with the nature of 'taste', and 'the concern to get at this elusive irrational phenomenon with rational means was urgent'.[16]

During the Renaissance some attempts were made to codify the irrational or emotional elements thought to be contained in music, by appealing back to the principles of Rhetoric, developed for oratory by the Greeks. Rhetoric was based on an elaborate set of rules, whereby an audience's response could supposedly be manipulated and predicted. Techniques of constructing a speech aimed to create desired responses:

The rediscovery in 1416 of Quintilian's 'Institutio oratoria' provided one of the primary sources on which the growing union between rhetoric and music was based in the 16th century.[17]

From the late 15th century onwards classical rhetoric was a central part of European educational curricula, in Catholic, and post-Reformation Protestant countries. The article on Rhetoric in New Grove states that:

This universal development had a profound impact on composers' attitudes to text-bound music, sacred as well as secular, and led to new musical styles and forms of which the madrigal and opera are only the most obvious products.[18]

Medieval thought linked music with the sciences of mathematics, geometry and astronomy, while also asserting 'emotional' or spiritual correlations for certain formal musical elements. The association of triple time with the Holy Trinity, for example, was a simple mathematical correlation, ascribing more

---

15 Ibid, p6
16 Ibid, p8
17 'Rhetoric', *New Grove*, Vol 15
18 Ibid

devotional attributes to triple time than to duple time. As an extension of this, the modes were thought to have powerful associations. The Locrian mode, which begins on B natural, was considered a 'forbidden' mode, because of the F-B tritone, an uncomfortable interval to sing. It led to the idea that it constituted a Satanic force – known as 'diabolus in musica'.

Because liturgical music combines words with religious messages, the 'meanings' and purposes of sacred music always seem to be clear. By the eighteenth century, the Churches (Catholic and Protestant) were no longer the sole patrons and controllers of musical forms and practices, and the separation between vocal and instrumental music was well under way. Music production, distribution and consumption was increasingly secularised. Publishing, concert and opera-going, amateur music making, the rise of the secular 'middling class' audience, put music in the commercial market-place.

While opera combined words and music in secular narratives, rather than for liturgical purposes, instrumental music developed independent forms. Dalhaus rightly points out that instrumental music had existed in its own right for some 150 years, but now there was a different imperative to explore the nature of 'meaning' in, and of, instrumental music. Musical elements were being codified, entailing consistency of clefs, designated orchestration, the awareness of national styles (the great Franco-Italian debate), and, more broadly-based and thorough-going than before, attempts to define the 'emotional' element in music.

German writers explored a 'Doctrine of the Affections'. Johann Mattheson developed the concept of a 'language of tones as if it were real speech'.[19] These 'moods', or feelings, were attributed to pitch, key characteristics, timbre and systems of tuning. Rita Steblin cogently describes the history of this process,[20] from the

19   Mattheson, Johann, *Der Vollkommene Capellmeister,* 1739
20   Steblin, Rita, *A History of Key Characteristics in the 18th and early 19th Centuries* (UMI Research Press, 1983)

starting point of the way 'ethical meanings were attributed to the church modes'[21] through to Mattheson.

The 'Doctrine' could not – self-evidently – work. As Dalhaus (almost impatiently) points out:

> *It was assumed that a piece of music always asserted the same effect. If anyone noticed that this assumption did not fit, then the old doctrine of the four temperaments was invoked to explain exceptions from the rule: whoever failed to recognise cheerful music as such must be a melancholic type who assimilated into his own dismal constitution everything he heard. The doctrines of the affections and of the temperaments mutually shielded each other against disproof by experience.*[22]

Efforts to relate music, emotion and meaning continued to be played out into the nineteenth century by philosophers and musicologists. Hegel, according to Dalhaus, argued for the supremacy of vocal music, because the text brought with it identifiable, definite meanings. Dalhaus reminds us that:

> *... listeners searched in Beethoven's symphonies for esoteric programmes rather than grasping them as evidence of a transition to the hegemony of instrumental music.*[23]

Musical Aestheticians

✿ EDUARD HANSLICK (1854) ✿

Eduard Hanslick was a professor at Vienna University, and his book, *The Beautiful in Music*, was published in 1854.[24] It was first translated into English in 1891 by Gustav Cohen, who comments that the book was a product of the 'irreconcilable antagonism' of

---

21   Ibid, p19
22   Dalhaus, ibid, p25
23   Ibid, p29
24   Hanslick, Eduard, *The Beautiful in Music*, trans. Gustav Cohen (Novello, 1891)

schools of musical thought of the time. Hanslick's book was part of efforts to make sense of a dualism in Western thought: the split between intellect and emotion, and the attempt to handle both of these aspects of the human mind by appeal to rational discourse.

The development of the natural sciences had opened up enormous possibilities for intellectual speculation. At the same time, early nineteenth-century Romantic poets stressed the importance of heightened emotional states in the process of writing, and this fed into the view that music came about as a result of spontaneous emotional creativity and equally spontaneous emotional responses on the part of an audience.

Hanslick takes the relationship between music and emotion seriously, combining it with other considerations. He is emphatic that: ' ... there is no causal nexus between a musical composition and the feelings it may excite, as the latter vary with our experience and impressibility.'[25] In other words, there is no 'feeling' or emotion immanent in the music – notes and performance – itself. The emotions – whatever they may be – are variable and associative.

The imagination of the composer creates the music, and the imagination of the listener 'contemplates it with intelligence'.[26] The 'beauty' that exists, he says 'affects not our feelings, but the organ of pure contemplation, our imagination'.[27]

Unlike the writers on 'Affects' in music, Hanslick sees meaning as contextual, and dependent on 'the meanings we ourselves attach to them':

... in like manner, the first elements of music, such as the various keys, chords and timbres have severally a character of their own.[28]

Hanslick describes music as 'the most ethereal of all arts',

---

25   Ibid, p25
26   Ibid, p21
27   Ibid, p20
28   Ibid, p39

commenting that 'Poetry, sculpture and painting are, in point of well-grounded aesthetic treatment, far in advance of music'.[29] He advocates a materialist approach, arguing that:

... the method obtaining in natural science be followed, at least in the sense of dealing with the things themselves, in order to determine what is permanent and objective in them ... [30]

The purpose of pursuing a 'scientific' investigation of music is to find out 'by what laws of nature it is governed, what the canons of art are that determine its form'.[31] Hanslick is not interested, however, in a mathematically based analysis as the source of an understanding of beauty: 'the beautiful in music is totally independent of mathematics'.[32]

When Hanslick calls for intellectual and scientific rigour, he resorts to metaphor and analogy:

As music has no prototype in nature and expresses no definite conceptions, we are compelled to speak of it either in dry, technical terms, or in the language of poetic fiction. All the fantastic descriptions, characterisations, and periphrases are either metaphorical or false. What in any other art is still descriptive, is in music already figurative.[33]

As a result of the genuine difficulty of matching verbal language to a non-verbal art, he uses the metaphor of an architectural arabesque, which expresses his view of 'a perfect whole'[34] made out of parts. Another image is the kaleidoscope where

... ever changing tints and forms ... all logically connected with each other, yet all novel in their effect forming, as it were, a complete

---

29   Ibid, p16
30   Ibid, p16
31   Ibid, p19
32   Ibid, p91
33   Ibid, p70
34   Ibid, p67

self-subsistent whole.[35]

Even while Hanslick reaches for a 'scientific law', along with the use of metaphor, he is drawn to his roots in Romantic thinking, which held very powerful mystical ideas about the muse, genius, inspiration and creativity:

> ... *the logic in music, which produces in us a feeling of satisfaction, rests on certain elementary laws of nature, which govern both the human organism and the phenomena of sound. It is, above all, the primordial law of 'harmonic progression' which, similarly to the curve line in painting and sculpture is the germ of development in its main forms and the – unfortunately almost unexplained cause of the link which connects the various musical phenomena.*

> *All musical elements are in some occult manner connected with each other by certain natural affinities, and since rhythm, melody and harmony are under their invisible sway, the music created by man* (sic) *must conform to them.*[36]

Words such as 'occult', 'primitive', 'primordial' and the phrase 'the occult and primitive affinities of the musical elements', collide with mysticism to explain the power/meaning of music. The 'laws' and the means with which to express and understand them, are thus, at best, elusive.

Hanslick was a product of his time in another way. The nineteenth-century idea of evolutionary progress was applied to tonal music as representing a high stage of development. He dismisses Greek music as not being a valid art because of:

> *The lack of harmony, the poverty of the melody within the extremely narrow limits of the recitative ... (it) was always used ... with poetry, dancing and pantomimic representation, in other words as an adjunct of other arts.*[37]

---

35   Ibid, p68
36   Ibid, p71
37   Ibid, p132

The building blocks of tonal structure, therefore, come close to attaining the status of a law of nature

... melody and harmony, our intervals and our scale, the division into major and minor ... and the equal temperament without which our music (the West European) would be impossible, are slowly gained triumphs of the human mind.

Nature has given man but the organs and the inclination to sing, together with the faculty to create a musical system having its roots in the most simple relations of sound. Only the latter (the triad, harmonic progression) will ever remain the indestructible foundation upon which all future development must rest.[38]

This 'progressive' view of human development puts Western European man (sic) at the top of the evolutionary pyramid:

It is beyond question that the action of music was far more direct in the case of ancient races than it is with us, because mankind is much more easily impressed by elemental forces in a primitive state of culture than later on, when intellectual consciousness and the faculty of reflection have attained a higher degree of maturity.[39]

Hanslick addresses emotion in a number of ways. First, he comments on the way an excess of emotion can get in the way of the ability to compose music. His 'proof' is based on some misogynistic assumptions – another example of the way he is a product of his Victorian times:

... women, who by nature are highly emotional beings, have achieved nothing as composers. The cause, apart from the general reasons why women are less capable of mental achievements, is the plastic element in musical compositions which like sculpture and architecture, though in a different manner, imposes on us the necessity of keeping ourselves free from all subjective feelings. If the composing of music depended upon the intensity and vividness of

---

38   Ibid, p147
39   Ibid, p131

our feelings, the complete want of female composers as against the numerous authoresses and female painters, would be difficult to account for. It is not the feeling but a specifically musical and technically trained aptitude that enables us to compose.[40]

An addition to a pyramid of stereotypes provides further indication of the 'superiority' of northern Europeans:

The monopoly of the soprano in the Italian school is mainly due to the mental indolence of the Italian people, who are incapable of that assiduous fixing of the attention so characteristic of Northern races ... [41]

Hanslick's Western Eurocentric world view infuses his view of nature and its laws: 'nature' only comes into valid existence with diatonic, triadic tonality. Contemplation and the appreciation of beauty in music are open only to those who are musically trained (not women, and therefore a male elite), who are Northern Europeans (and hence not subject to the excessive passions of either the Southern Europeans or 'savages'). Only white men are really able to compose, because women are mentally limited and too emotional.

Along with these prejudices, the concern with, and about, emotion threads through his arguments:

Music operates on our emotional faculty with greater intenseness and rapidity than the product of any other art.[42]

However, it does so in a way that is entirely dependent:

... upon physiological conditions. The material element, which in all aesthetic enjoyment is at the root of the intellectual one, is greater in music than in any other one ... Music, through its immateriality the most ethereal art, and yet the most sensuous one through its play of forms ... exhibits ... a strong affinity for the nerves, these equally

40   Ibid, p101
41   Ibid, p136
42   Ibid, p107

mysterious links in the invisible telegraphic connection between mind and body.[43]

The most essential part, the physiological process by which the sensation of sound is converted into a feeling, a state of mind, is unexplained and will ever remain so.[44]

... all this lies beyond the mysterious bridge which no philosopher has ever crossed ... the connection between mind and body.[45]

What is 'unknown' extends to the source of the act of composition, and the Romantic 'inspiration':

Thanks to that primitive and mysterious power, whose mode of action will forever be hidden from us, a theme, a melody, flashes on the composer's mind. The origin of this first germ cannot be explained but must simply be accepted as a fact.[46]

Additionally, the genesis of a composition cannot be understood from the composer's biography, or from the composer's 'intentions':

Aesthetically speaking, it is utterly indifferent whether Beethoven really did associate all his works with certain ideas. We do not know them, and as far as the composition is concerned, they do not exist.[47]

There is one area where Hanslick is not in doubt about the place of emotion: in the act of performance:

The player has the privilege of venting directly through his (sic) instrument the feeling by which he is swayed at the time, and to breathe into his performance passionate excitement, ardent longing, buoyant strength and joy. The mere physical impulse which directly communicated the inward tremor as the fingers touch the strings, as the hand draws the bow, or as the vocal chords vibrate in song,

---

43   Ibid, p109
44   Ibid, p116
45   Ibid, p119
46   Ibid, p73
47   Ibid, p85

enables the executant to pour forth his inmost feelings. His subjectiveness thus makes itself directly heard in the music and is not merely the silent prompter ... The piece of music is worked out by the composer, but it is the performance which we enjoy. Thus the active and emotional principle occurs in the act of reproduction, which draws the electric spark from a mysterious source and directs it towards the heart of the listener ... it is the spirit of the player which is revealed.[48]

Indirectly, this again confirms the absence of discernible intrinsic emotion in the music itself.

What, then, according to Hanslick, 'is' music?

... its nature is specifically musical ... By this we mean that the beautiful is not contingent upon, or in need of any subject introduced from without, but that it consists wholly of sounds artistically combined.[49]

Music expresses 'musical ideas' and 'The essence of music is sound and motion'.[50] From here he addresses the issue of 'representation':

A certain class of ideas ... is quite susceptible of being adequately expressed ... audible changes of strength, motion and ratio: the ideas of intensity waxing and diminishing; of motion fastening and lingering; of ingeniously complex and simple progression.[51]

... it may reproduce the motion accompanying physical action, according to its momentum: speed, slowness, strength, weakness, increasing, decreasing intensity. But motion is only one of the concomitants of feeling, not the feeling itself.[52]

'*... music consists of successions and forms of sound, and these*

---

48   Ibid, pp106-7
49   Ibid, p66
50   Ibid, p67
51   Ibid, pp35-36
52   Ibid, p38

alone constitute the subject.' [53]

Hanslick's primary aim was to remove music from the assumption that its only, and mystical, purpose is to express and evoke feelings. For music to be an object worthy of philosophical and aesthetic inquiry, he contests the excessive focus on the concept of 'emotions' as the 'subject' of music, as the content 'put into it', as it were, by the composer.

Hanslick's book encapsulates the contradictory nature of materialism and idealism. He acknowledges the autonomy of the material musical text, the physical relationship between performer and instrument. However, because he rejects the immanence of emotion in music, he invests the scientific object (which he has successfully isolated) and its analysis, with spirituality, with the divine and unknowable, with the concept of inspiration, to lead him to a Romantic definition of beauty.

However, the book's central contradiction is also its success; polemically, Hanslick clears away misconceptions in order to see what the object is that needs analysis – the musical work. Any emotional relationship with the music is extrinsic and associative.

❧ BENEDETTO CROCE (1913) ❧

Benedetto Croce's anti-materialist line is, by implication, in opposition to Hanslick, and is clear from the start of his *Guide to Aesthetics*, published in 1913. He asks: 'What is Art?', responding that 'art is vision or intuition'[54] as against:

... anything which goes under the name of 'physical'. This error of materialising art has already made a dent upon popular thought.[55]

He rejects the idea that art has any utilitarian or social function, denying:

---

53   Ibid, p162
54   Croce, Benedetto, *Guide to Aesthetics* (Bobbs Merrill, 1965), p8
55   Ibid, p9

... that artists contribute to the public education of the lower classes, the reinforcing of national or warlike spirit of a people, the spreading of ideas of a modest and industrious life ... [56]

His definition of art as 'intuition', also assumes that it cannot provide 'conceptual knowledge'.[57] While he doesn't discuss music directly, he 'uses' music as a means of defining art, via a metaphor from Walter Pater:

'All art (constantly) aspires towards the condition of music.' Concerning which it would be necessary to state more exactly that all the arts are music, if thereby we wish to give emphasis to the emotional origin of artistic images ... [58]

This makes it sound as if music equals emotion. However, this isn't an idea he pursues. Despite his resistance to the 'physical', Croce cannot get away from the fact that art can only come into being in some material form:

A thought is not for us thought unless it is formulated into words. Neither is a musical fancy unless it is made concrete through sounds.[59]

... this apparent transformation of intuitions into physical things (is) ... exactly analogous to the apparent transformation of needs and economic work into things and goods.[60]

Still resisting the potential towards materialism, Croce believes that an artist expresses the 'self',[61] the 'spirit', claiming that any relationship with the commercial world is damaging. Any artist who has:

... one eye on art and the other on the spectator, the publisher, the

56   Ibid, p13
57   Ibid, p14
58   Ibid, p26
59   Ibid, p34
60   Ibid, p37
61   Ibid, p57

impresario ... if they are not careful about guarding themselves against such things, they introduce into their work sonorous but empty verses, inaccuracies, dissonances, discords.[62]

According to Croce, only the critic can identify the intuition which constitutes true 'art':

Thus all art criticism may be reduced to the following very brief proposition: 'there is a work of art – a' or 'there is not a work of art – a'[63]

Croce's critic has a role of great cultural and ideological significance:

... art criticism, when it is truly aesthetic or historical through its very process, develops into criticism of life.[64]

Croce's evaluation of the critic is close to the Leavisite paradigm, in which great art is mediated by the critic/teacher to convey the 'criticism of life' contained in the work of art. F.R. Leavis and his wife, Q.D. Leavis, took up this idea, developing it in their literary publication, *Scrutiny,* in the 1930s. Their approach influenced the later study of literature, as well as having an influence on discussions about music, as we shall see later.

✎ R.G. COLLINGWOOD (1937) ✎

Collingwood, unlike Croce, is as concerned with practitioners and consumers as he is with philosophical disquisition:

For I do not think of aesthetic theory as an attempt to investigate and expound eternal verities concerning the nature of an eternal object called Art, but as an attempt to reach, by thinking, the solution of certain problems arising out of the situation in which artists find

---

62   Ibid, p67
63   Ibid, p74
64   Ibid, p81

themselves here and now ... [65]

Collingwood begins with a historical account of art:

Art in medieval Latin meant any special form of book learning, such as grammar and logic, magic or astrology. That is still its meaning in the time of Shakespeare ... But the Renaissance, first in Italy and then elsewhere re-established the old meaning, and the Renaissance artists, like those of the ancient world, did actually think of themselves as craftsmen. It was not until the 17th century that the problems and conceptions of aesthetics began to be disentangled from those of technique or the philosophy of craft. [66]

During the 1930s, both sides of the political spectrum tussled over the moral, social, spiritual, emotional function of art and the artist. The mass media were being established: broadcasting - radio – the gramophone, the potentials of television, and, of course – film. Collingwood makes the distinction between 'high' and 'low' art, echoing Hanslick's 'uncultured masses' in his dismissal of the mass media as 'entertainment'. [67]

Collingwood has no problem acknowledging the fact that art is a commodity, a part of material, social production:

To the economist, art presents the appearance of a specialised group of industries; the artist is a producer, his audience consumers who pay him for benefits ultimately definable in terms of the states of mind which his productivity enables them to enjoy. [68]

Addressing the issue of representation in music, Collingwood also stresses the associative – even if it is speculative – rather than the intrinsic presence of emotion:

... music, in order to be representative, need not copy the noises made by bleating sheep, an express locomotive at speed or a rattle in

65   Collingwood, R.G., *The Principles of Art* (OUP, 1937), pvi
66   Ibid, p6
67   Ibid, p11
68   Ibid, p19

the throat of a dying man. The pianoforte accompaniment of Brahms' song 'Feldeinsamkeit' ... does make noises which evoke a feeling remarkably like that which a man feels on such an occasion.[69]

Significantly, Collingwood expresses a romantic regret about a lost golden rural age and art:

Until close on the end of the 19th century the rustic population had an art of its own, rooted in the distant past but still alive with creative vigour: songs and dances, seasonal feasts and dramas and pageantry, all of magical significance and all organically connected with agricultural work. In a single generation this was wiped out by the Education Act of 1870 which was one stage in the slow destruction of English rural life by the dominant industrial and commercial class.[70]

The idea that the Education Act of 1870 had a destructive effect is, at the very least, odd. Like Croce, Collingwood privileges 'art in the head' – a mystical notion, which denies the material reality of art:

... what is written or printed on music-paper is not the tune. It is only something which when studied intelligently will enable others to construct the tune for themselves in their own heads.[71]

Collingwood's ideal is a kind of telepathy, communicated via printed music plus performance. The idea of art-in-the-composer's-head, conveyed to the art-in-the-listener's-head, is a spiritual justification for Collingwood's view of art as non-material, though still somehow expressing emotion:

By creating for ourselves an imaginary experience or activity, we express our emotions; and this is what we call art.[72]

... formalistic theories of art, popular though they have been and

69   Ibid, p56
70   Ibid, p102
71   Ibid, p135
72   Ibid, p151

are, have no relevance to art proper ... [73]

Collingwood suggests that the imagination mediates between the 'object' and response:

... imagination is a distinct level of experience intermediate between sensation and intellect, the point at which the life of thought makes contact with the life of purely physical experience.[74]

He 'explains' art/music by analogy with language. If, as he says, 'Art must be language':[75]

... the aesthetic experience or artistic activity, is the experience of expressing one's emotions; and that which expresses them is the total imaginative activity called indifferently language or art. This is art proper.[76]

He compares verbal language, spoken and written, with music, written and performed:

Speech ... is essentially a system of gestures made with the lungs and larynx and the cavities of the mouth and nose ... writing ... can represent only a small part of the spoken sound, where pitch and stress, tempo and rhythm, are almost entirely ignored ... The written or printed book is only a series of hints, elliptical as the neumes of Byzantine music, from which the reader thus works out for himself (sic) the speech-gestures which alone have the gift of expression.[77]

All the different kinds of language have a relation of this kind to bodily gesture ... Instrumental music has a similar relation to silent movements of the larynx, gestures of the player's hand, and real or imaginary movements as of the dancing, in the audience. Every kind of language is in this way a specialised form of bodily gesture, and in

---

73   Ibid, p142
74   Ibid, p215
75   Ibid, p273
76   Ibid, p275
77   Ibid, p243

this sense it may be said that the dance is the mother of all languages.[78]

The language of total bodily gesture is thus the motor side of our total imaginative experience.[79]

This dialectical understanding of the nature of communication, for which language is a metaphor, is perhaps the most important core of Collingwood's venture into the social relations of performance. Finally, he echoes Carr:

The musician did not invent his scale or his instruments; even if he invents a new scale or a new instrument, he is only modifying what he has learnt from others.[80]

An awareness of the importance of historic legacies leads Collingwood to concur with one element of the early music revival. If the 'arts are to flourish again as they have flourished in the past',[81] then stage directions and ... markings in scores must be removed.

✦ ROGER SCRUTON (1983) ✦

Scruton pays tribute to Hanslick's perception that:

... the theory of expression in all its forms ... means nothing until accompanied by an analysis of musical understanding.[82]

It would seem to follow that an artistic medium which, like music, can neither represent objects nor convey specific thoughts about them is logically debarred from expressing them. Such was Hanslick's argument, and it is marked, like the rest of his short but influential treatise, by a philosophical seriousness and competence that have few rivals in the field of musical aesthetics.[83]

78   Ibid, p243-4
79   Ibid, p247
80   Ibid, p316
81   Ibid, p328
82   Scruton, Roger, *The Aesthetic Understanding* (Carcanet, 1983), p35
83   Ibid, p58

Hanslick's argument is rather more sophisticated than that, since he adduces context and cultural difference to show how 'meaning' and 'emotion' become attached to music, rather than being intrinsic to it. Scruton claims that, even towards the end of the twentieth century, the debates were far from over:

By shifting from terms like 'representation' and 'description' to the vocabulary of human expression, critics and philosophers have hoped to locate an idea of content that will be compatible with music's status as an abstract art ... To put it more trenchantly: if music has a content, how can that content be described? It was thus that Hanslick posed the problem, and despite subsequent studies, the problem remains roughly as he posed it.[84]

MALCOLM BUDD (1985)

Malcolm Budd concurs with Hanslick that music is unable to 'represent' emotions or thoughts directly, but that it can convey the 'dynamic properties' of emotions.[85]

Budd deploys Freudian ideas of pleasure and pain, to relate concepts of satisfaction and dissatisfaction to tonality. Consonance and dissonance supposedly correspond to these two kinds of sensation – abutting on the possibility of comparing the effects of music to sexuality, though Budd does not articulate this explicitly.

NICHOLAS COOK (1992)

Cook, like Hanslick and Scruton, draws attention to the role of the critic in enlightening the 'informed listener', in a way which was central to the pioneers of twentieth-century literary criticism, as we shall see later. Like Hanslick, he dismisses the usefulness of the notion of 'intention':

---

84   Ibid, p77
85   Budd, Malcolm, *Music and the Emotions* (Routledge, 1985), p27

... it is not really the point to ask whether or not his ideas correspond to what Milton intended, because Milton is dead and what matters now is the aesthetic experience of Milton's text to which Leavis's interpretation may lead the reader. In the same way as Hanslick argued: 'aesthetically speaking, it is utterly indifferent whether Beethoven really did associate all his works with certain ideas'.[86]

Nicholas Cook co-edited one of the most stimulating collections which has come out of the New Musicology, in *Rethinking Music* (1999).[87]

Conclusion

These surveys present Hanslick's most important arguments about music and meaning, along with some of the ways he has been considered by some musicologists in the twentieth century. Hanslick's achievement was to separate, for analytical purposes, the various 'moments' in the life of a piece of music, in order to focus attention on the work itself – a materialist approach, which presaged the development of formalist analysis.

The effect of this was to break with the legacy of the Doctrine of Affects, which tried to 'prove' that the formal and technical elements of music intrinsically 'contained' emotion. However, Hanslick did not deny the fact that expression and emotion have an active relationship with music. He asserted that they were contextual and associative, and that is also one of the central arguments of this book.

In his discussion of emotion and expression, Hanslick was addressing what we would call 'interpretation', and this infuses his view of what is involved for the instrumental performer. Because his focus is on the work itself, while acknowledging the importance of composer attribution, he is clear that whether or not the

86   Cook, Nicholas, *Imagination and Culture* (OUP, 1992), p173
87   Cook, Nicholas and Everist, Mark, *Rethinking Music* (OUP, 1999)

composer's 'intentions' could be known, they are not relevant to an understanding of the musical work.

CHAPTER TWO

Music, Emotion and Meaning

ATTEMPTS TO EXPLORE the relationship between music and its expression (one form of interpretation), and emotion are really about the content of music; what it might be 'about', and what it might 'mean'. Given that music-on-the-page becomes music-in-performance, the issue of what the music is doing, and how it does it (another form of interpretation), becomes important. The issues overlap, and dissecting them for analysis is not always straightforward.

✒ ROGER SCRUTON (1983) ✒

Hanslick and others have argued that music cannot and does not represent extra-musical elements directly. Scruton redirects the question about representation (ie, mimetic content) to audience appreciation – the equivalent in literary discussions to 'reader response':

We are not concerned to show that music can or cannot represent objects. We are attempting to show rather that the question whether music is representational is a question about the appreciation of music, and not a question about music's structure.[88]

However, Scruton puts appreciation aside in favour of discussing expression:

Expression where it exists ... is integral to the aesthetic character of a piece of music, and must not be confused with any accidental

88 Scruton, Roger, *The Aesthetic Understanding* (Carcanet, 1983), p71

relation to the listener.[89]

> ... *there are no **definite** rules in music, no rules of the form, 'if the music has features A, B, C, then it will be expressive'.*[90]

With no clarity about what is 'expressive', how it inheres in music, or how it can be shown by musical features (A, B and C) for Scruton, appreciation is a matter of 'intuition', not capable of being described in words. This intuitive grasp enables the 'music lover' to hear and recognise the difference between the music of different historical periods, and by different composers:

> *We can indeed hear the historical relations between these composers – hear for example the Handelian elements in Mozart's arias, hear the stylistic negation of Bach's counterpoint in the chordal style of his son: and so on.*[91]

Clearly, the above abilities are only likely to be available to someone experientially and technically educated in the sounds and formal elements of musical composition, along with a knowledge of musical history and individual composers. In other words, only the musically informed person, who is part of the collusive 'we', can 'appreciate' classical music. Such appreciation depends on social situation and specific training. By implication, it supposedly excludes members of an audience who know nothing *about* music, but like listening to it.

Scruton is hostile to more expansive thinking about music:

> *It is wrong to **claim** that there is an historical process that we understand better than we understand this one ... when faced by some minor work of Telemann, Stamitz or Spohr, we should have little difficulty either in dating it, or in showing its stylistic relation to the principal musical manifestations of its period.*

> ~~This crystal~~ clear segment of musical history would become

---

89   Ibid, pp59-60
90   Ibid, p51
91   Ibid, p174

obscure at once, were we to look outside it to the social and economic determinants which, on one view, constitute the true explanation of cultural phenomena. We should have to relate Bach's position as a Lutheran Kapellmeister in a bourgeois town, to Haydn's life at the Esterhazy court, and to Beethoven's attempts to live without patronage in a burgeoning modern city. We should have to be clear about the economic transitions from late 17th-century mercantile capitalism in Germany, to post-revolutionary industrialism in Austria; and so on. Let us cut the story short: we do not understand those things and maybe we never will. We do understand the history of music. So the history of music has autonomy. If we start to play the game of the 'socio-economic' context we end up by misunderstanding music.[92]

For someone so hostile to materialism (and, by implication, to the New Musicology), Scruton describes the position extremely well. Even if one acknowledges the discrete history of music, the way is still open to consider how its possible 'meanings' might relate to history, and to the art of performance.

✺ TERRY EAGLETON (1976) ✺

Literary and cultural critic, Terry Eagleton, provides a corrective to Scruton. Although he writes about literature, his arguments can apply to music:

Marxist criticism is part of a large body of theoretical analysis which aims to understand ideologies - the ideas, values and feelings by which men (sic) experience their societies at various times.[93]

*Marxist criticism is not merely a 'sociology of literature (**music**)' ... Its aim is to explain the literary work (**music**) more fully; and this means a sensitive attention to its forms, styles and meanings.*[94]

---

92   Ibid, p174-5
93   Eagleton, Terry, *Marxism and Literary Criticism* (Methuen, 1976), pviii
94   Ibid, p3

*Literary **(musical)** works are not mysteriously inspired, or explicable simply in terms of their authors' psychology. They are forms of perception, particular ways of seeing the world which is the social mentality or ideology of an age.*[95]

While literature and music are not identical, questions about whether literature 'reflects' reality are akin to debates about whether music can 'represent' something (emotion, the programmatic, etc) which is extra-musical, and which derives from other human perceptions, feelings, experiences and phenomena in the world:

... art is a form of social production ... We may see literature as a text, but we may also see it as a social activity, a form of social and economic production which exists alongside and interrelates with, other such forms.[96]

... art, like any other form of production, depends upon certain techniques of production – certain modes of painting etc ... these techniques are part of the productive forces of art, the stage of development of artistic production; and they involve a set of social relations between the artistic producer and ... audience.[97]

Eagleton moves on to discuss drama/music as performance arts:

A dramatic performance is clearly more than a 'reflection' of the dramatic text; on the contrary ... it is a transformation of the text into a unique product, which involves re-working it in accordance with the specific demands and conditions of theatrical performance.[98]

This schematic presentation of two very different approaches to understanding and analysing music shows there are fruitful possibilities in a historical and contextual approach, which still

---

95   Ibid, p6
96   Ibid, p60
97   Ibid, p61
98   Ibid, p51

allows for accounts of the 'internal evolution' of musical forms, styles and author/composership. This enables a wider scope and a fuller comprehension of where and how 'meanings' may connect with music, and how they are communicated.

✤ LEONARD MEYER (1956) ✤

Leonard Meyer argues for a clear theory of meaning, which he believes is inherent in tonal music.[99] First, *pace* Hanslick:

> *... not only does music use no linguistic signs but, on one level at least, it operates as a closed system, that is, it employs no signs or symbols referring to the non-musical world of objects, concepts and human desires.*[100]

> *... unlike a closed, non-referential mathematical system, music is said to communicate emotional and aesthetic meanings as well as purely intellectual ones.*[101]

In order to reconcile these paradoxical propositions, Meyer echoes Scruton's argument about the informed listener, and the need for a consciously shared musical culture. The assumption appears to be that only such people can discern emotional and other meanings in the music. This depends upon:

> *... the absolute necessity of a common universe of discourse in art. For without a set of gestures common to the social group, and without common habit responses to those gestures, no communication whatsoever would be possible. Communication depends upon, presupposes and arises out of the universe of discourse which in the aesthetics of music is called style.*[102]

True to post-Hanslick form, Meyer largely uses tonal and post-

---

99   Meyer, Leonard B., *Emotion and Meaning in Music* (University of Chicago Press, 1956).
100   Ibid, pvii
101   Ibid, pvii
102   Ibid, p42

tonal music as examples of conveyed stylistic meanings. For him, certainly, the subtleties of surprise and deviation from (presumably, tonal) expectation produce significance, or some sort of meaning/affect, although it is still not at all clear what this is, whether it is fixed or how it is conveyed. He uses the term 'style' in two senses, the individual, and the cultural, which correspond in linguistics to 'dialect' and 'idiolect':

> *Bach and Beethoven represent different styles within a single style system, while Mozart and Machaut employ different style systems.*[103]

Acknowledging the cultural nature of musical discourse, Meyer develops his theory of meaning/affect, implying a universalism of response:

> *The patterns of style ... made, modified and discarded by musicians. What remains constant is the nature of human responses and the principles of pattern perception, the ways in which the mind operating within the framework of a learned style, selects and organises the sense data presented to it.*[104]

> *Just as communicative behaviour tends to become conventionalised for the sake of more efficient communication, so the musical communication of moods and sentiments tends to become standardised. Thus, particular musical devices – melodic figures, harmonic progression, or rhythmic relationship, become formulas which indicate a culturally codified mood or sentiment.*[105]

Such codification varies from culture to culture:

> *... in the West death is usually depicted by slow tempi and low ranges, while in certain African tribes it is portrayed in frenzied musical activity.*[106]

---

103 Ibid, p64
104 Ibid, p73
105 Ibid, p267
106 Ibid, p259

Meyer's main focus is on Western, diatonic music. He applies Gestalt theory, which argues that perception builds patterns out of stimuli, basing these on expectation, deviation, tension and release, 'very similar to those experienced in real life' – in other words, meanings are associative:

The greater the build-up of suspense, of tension, the greater the emotional release upon resolution.[107]

The unspoken analogy with sexual/erotic response is clear, but unprovable. In expanding on the concept of 'expectation' and 'deviation', Meyer refers to 'expressive' devices such as tempo (rubato), vibrato (as a historically variable pitch-deviation), and even ornamentation:

We must revise our attitude towards ornamentation. Ornaments are of the essence of music ... Indeed, since music is architectonic, it is possible to consider even the largest section of a composition as being essentially ornamental.[108]

He therefore claims that baroque ornamentation resulted in a 'connection between ornamentation and affective, expressive experience',[109] as embellishments delay the explicit arrival of the 'expected'. In fact, ornamentation does not delay anything, since it operates within given rhythmic structures.

The difficulty is that, however attractive Meyer's propositions are, without examples and genuine proof as to how particular 'meanings' can derive from specific moments in musical form, his arguments are little more than a latter-day Doctrine of Affects.

EDWARD CONE (1968)

Cone addresses performance directly, suggesting that music is 'framed' as a temporal event, preceded by an expectant silence. It

107 Ibid, p28
108 Ibid, p205
109 Ibid, p207

begins with an upbeat, which might be a single note, or, as he says, 'an introduction is an expanded upbeat':

A proper musical performance must ... be a dramatic, even a theatrical event, presenting as it does an action with a beginning, a middle and an end – hence an action of a certain completeness in itself. This dramatic quality must be present whether the performance is entirely private, as when one reads the music quietly, or plays it over to oneself, or whether there is a public ... [110]

He offers an interesting theory of musical response: the 'synoptic comprehension', which 'either recognises a unity in what is perceived or else imposes one on it'[111] and the 'immediate apprehension',[112] which he says is the more realistic state of things, since 'no mind ever perceives a continuum as a whole'.[113] This is a two-tier, time-determined matter: what is appreciated in the immediacy of performance, and what may result over time, memory and greater familiarity with the music:

The compositions that are ultimately the most satisfying are those that invite and reward both modes of perception.[114]

There are so many undefined terms: 'pleasing', 'interesting', 'rewarding', all whetting the appetite for precision. The idea of two time-determined modes of comprehension and appreciation are true for any art: there is the first, fresh experience of the unknown, and the kinds of responses which develop over time, greater knowledge and understanding. It is not clear what might be specific to music.

⚓ ROGER SESSIONS (1974) ⚓

Roger Sessions addresses performance as a composer, rather

---

110   Cone, Edward, *Musical Form and Musical Performance* (Norton, 1968), p14
111   Ibid, p88
112   Ibid, p89
113   Ibid, p91
114   Ibid, p96

than a musicologist.[115] Inevitably, he has an experiential, as well as a vested, interest in the relationship between composer and performer, who must discover:

... the musical gestures inherent in the composer's text and then reproducing them according to his (sic) *own lights.*[116]

Two central concepts are encapsulated in these lines: a) the composer's 'intentions', as revealed by the written music, and b) the 'interpretation', represented by what the performer brings to the realisation of the music.

According to Sessions, performance is:

... the result of a collaboration between the composer and a particular performer on a particular occasion.[117]

... composer, performer and listener each fulfil one of three separate functions in a totally creative process which was originally undifferentiated and which still is essentially indivisible.

The high degree of differentiation reached in the course of the development of music should not obscure the fact that in the last analysis composer and performer are not only collaborators in a common enterprise but participants in an essentially single experience.[118]

On the surface this may seem like an ideal, perhaps common sense, understanding. This is problematic. The term 'differentiation' is what one can also call the division of labour, in the process of composing, rehearsing and performing music, each of which takes place over an extended, and differentiated, period of time.

The 'single experience' Sessions refers to can apply to the

---

115   Sessions, Roger, *The Musical Experience of Composer, Performer, Listener* (Princeton University Press,1974)
116   Ibid, p78
117   Ibid, p85
118   Ibid, p5

performance, the moment when everything 'comes together', but that is the end of the process. The composer does not (generally) perform, the performer does not (generally) compose. They have very different relationships to the same piece of music. The concept of collaboration (*pace* Collingwood) conceals the complexity of the reality.

To this group Sessions adds the critic ('the listener who has become articulate')[119] into his circle of unity:

... the true role of critic ... is that of collaborator so to speak, in a common cultural effort in which composer and performer and listener all participate.[120]

The idea of a 'common' enterprise' and a 'single experience' is romantically attractive. However, it doesn't stand up conceptually or analytically, since each distinct role, matters of hierarchy, power, who makes decisions about performance and style cannot be collapsed into one seamless unity of time.

However, it is interesting that Sessions echoes Hanslick's notion that music can mirror dynamic properties which relate to more everyday activities. Unlike Meyer's suggestively erotic associations, Sessions has a simpler biologistic model for tension/release:

The drawing of breath is an act of cumulation, tension, which is then released by the alternative act of exhalation.[121]

It is unnecessary to seek scientific proof of this. We need only a clear analysis of ordinary experience... the speed with which we accomplish walking.[122]

The appeal to ordinary experience may well have an experiential reality, in that each person can decide for themselves which musical properties have emotional responses for them, but it

119   Ibid, p100
120   Ibid, p103
121   Ibid, p12
122   Ibid, p16

doesn't help us to understand the process any better.

❧ NICHOLAS COOK (1990) ❧

Nicholas Cook points out that there is a 'difference between how people think or talk about music on the one hand, and how it is experienced'. He claims that words 'distort the experiences that they are intended to represent'.[123] One could, of course, say that of any of the performance arts. However, it is a truism that discussing any art form has to take place using verbal language. Cook's remarks imply that any use of language will not be able to do justice to music. They are different discourses, and it is the relationship between them which is important. Like Scruton, Cook argues that those who partake in (and appreciate) music, must be educated and informed:

Like a number of other writers, mainly ethnomusicologists, I would argue that a musical culture is essentially a cognitive entity, in other words, that to define a musical culture means defining the things a people must know in order to understand, perform and create acceptable music in their culture.[124]

It is worth noting again that the above excludes listeners/ audience who may know little or nothing 'about' music, but who still gain much from it. On performance, Cook makes an analogy with reading:

... reading a book, then, is a performance in the sense of being a temporally extended process during which the text yields up its signification through being experienced by the reader; and if this is true of reading books then it is certainly no less true of reading music.[125]

Reading a book is clearly very different from 'reading music'.

---

123   Cook, Nicholas, *Music, Imagination and Culture* (OUP, 1990), p1
124   Ibid, p222
125   Ibid, p125

The first is a silent, one-to-one relationship between book and reader, the second form of reading goes through at least two stages: being 'lifted' off the page (ie, 'read') and then performed in either live or recorded form. Only then does it reach its audience – in mass form (concerts) or individual consumption through private listening.

Continuing the comparison with language, Cook looks briefly at ensemble playing:

> *... presumably what is involved is an entire network of relational exchanges that depend on the particular organisation of the music...a parallel with the rapport and give and take of people engaged in conversing together ...* [126]

Conversation is essentially improvisatory - unrehearsed, individuated, spontaneous. Musical rehearsal and performance, however, are group events, highly formalised, predetermined, with rhythmic coherence, and with simultaneous sound-making. The rapport between people can be superficially compared to any kind of group activity; however, each activity will have its own specific characteristics, dynamics and conventions.

❧ ANTHONY ROOLEY (1990) ❧

Anthony Rooley draws on considerable performance experience,[127] making proto-religious claims for the impact of performance:

> *Ritualised performances – in the concert hall ... channel our awareness because they are ritualised, but what we perceive there can illumine our daily lives.*[128]

> *Orpheus* [is] *the archetypal performer, receiving his inspiration*

---

126 Ibid, p.130-131
127 Rooley, Anthony, *Performance: Revealing the Orpheus Within* (Element Books, 1990)
128 Ibid, p.12

directly from the Divine.[129]

The appeal to Greek myth, God and a post-hippie mysticism infuse Rooley's diagrams in a proto-cabalistic way, aiming to show how performance works. At the centre is the 'source of creative energy'[130] with the performer and audience around it. Through this, Rooley reclaims a concept of hierarchy, which he says has gone 'rather out of fashion'.[131] A non-denominational 'God' presides, below whom is a middle-management level (my metaphor) soul, then the mind and the body.

Rooley's performer carries 'Orphic skills' – 'the performer, the priest, the healer, as well as the lover'.[132] Through identification with Orpheus, the performer can unite body and soul 'to a higher understanding', though it is not clear of what this understanding consists.[133]

Giving the performer a priest-like role, and arguing for performance to serve spiritual ends, demands a 'congregation':

The audience takes the lead from the performer ... [134] *Every time you enter the performing space, new discoveries are made, for you have, truly, never been in that time/space before ...* [135] *There is a moment to start which is in harmony with the performer, the audience, the space, the time. With experience that knowledge or sense of when to place the first sound or movement becomes ever more sure...*[136]

Performance, for Rooley, becomes 'meditation'.[137] The mystical rationale is primary, making the performer not only priest, but

129   Ibid, p3
130   Ibid, p24
131   Ibid, p27
132   Ibid, p100
133   Ibid, p108
134   Ibid, p49
135   Ibid, p50
136   Ibid, p51
137   Ibid, p52

God. The artist-god-turned-priest-performer makes music into the religious ritual in the concert space, which then becomes 'sacred'. In the swirl of mixes between Renaissance and modern imagery, the hippie and the religious, the performer is priest and mediator of the 'musica mundana' – the music of the spheres - to all us lay folk out there.

Conclusion

Each of the above writers has a serious commitment to exploring the relationship between music, emotion and meaning. It is clear, though not explicitly stated, that where these musicologists and performers claim 'meanings', they are, in all cases, associative, rather than intrinsic. Such representation – mimesis – as there is, derives from extrinsic cultural, physical and/or personal sources, or from the coincidence of dynamic elements (rhythm, pace), which might relate to anything at all outside the music.

Issues of interpretation are relevant across musical history, just as they are for dramatic performance. References to performance, however relatively minimal, open the way for a discussion about ways in which such conditions contribute to, or determine, the possible meanings of (rather than 'in') music.

INTERVAL

CHAPTER THREE

Music into Performance

A proper musical performance must ... be a dramatic, even a theatrical event, presenting as it does an action with a beginning, a middle and an end – hence an action of a certain completeness in itself. This dramatic quality must be present, whether the performance is entirely private, as when one reads the music quietly, or plays it over to oneself, or whether there is a public ... [138]

❧ TRAINING FOR PERFORMANCE ❧

AT THE OTHER end of the conceptual spectrum from discussions about the relationship between music and aesthetics, emotion and meaning, is the practical matter of training for performance.

While at Trinity College of Music, I interviewed four instrumental teachers, to see how they broached 'emotion', 'expression' and 'interpretation' with their students. Singers clearly have a text with clues to 'expressive' and dramatic tropes in performance, and vocal coaches for these will have approaches which take words into account, along with the music. However, I deliberately approached instrumental teachers to see how they might deal with the issues.

The Trinity teachers were Simon Young, piano (SY); Elizabeth Turnbull, strings (ET); Gilbert Berberian, guitar (GB) and Stephen Nagy, wind (SN). The quotes here are inevitably suggestive rather

---

138   Cone, Edward, op. cit., p14

than conclusive, and they highlight the chasm between questions asked by music aestheticians, and the preoccupations of those on the ground, as it were.

It is not that teachers don't think about the same questions, but that they have to think about them differently, with pedagogic implications for the students' training for performance: developing technique, style, attitudes towards the industry, the relationship between individual performance and ensemble work. While very few music students go on to be solo performers, the training of each instrumental student is on a one-to-one basis with their teacher, as if they are actually going to become soloists. Orchestral and ensemble 'training' take place elsewhere, with coaches/ conductors, building musical skills with the group as a whole.

☙ TECHNIQUE ❧

GB: *I say, 'The best I can do for you is to give you a technique, a tool you can use on your instrument to allow as free as possible expression of your musicality, and, above all, that which the music has to say. I spend a long time working on the hands.*

ET: *I feel to a large extent that any string player has to regard themselves physically as part of the instrument; technique is a means of being able to say what you want to say. It's a musical vocabulary, and like with any good computer, it's only as good as what you put into it. We're training what I call a learned instinct, so that when you see a message on a piece of music, your whole brain goes into gear and sends out responses. It's got to be so instinctive that it's like thinking of the words to express what you mean when you say a sentence.*

☙ INTERPRETATION ❧

SY: *They ought to try and find out as much as possible about a piece of music, before they start work on it; go through the thing in their heads, go through it on the page; they ought to be able to hear it.*

SN: *The first thing is the content. What do they think of a piece? It can be a dance, it can be a song, it can describe an animal, a mood. But it's got a title. It's got a meaning. You look for what the particular piece expresses.*

Obviously the social situation is important; is it played in a concert hall, in a ballroom? Is this an overture to an opera? Or is it harmonic music which was background music while people ate and drank?

✎ EXPRESSION ✎

ET: *You can't teach anyone to be a musician, you can lead them right up to that very moment and have given them all the ability to contact things in themselves, but if they don't put that final little bridge across the gap, you can't get in. It's between you and your maker, whoever that is.*

SY: *I think some people will never have it. In some cases it's a matter of drawing it out, because there's all sorts of reasons why it's being blocked. I think expressive is the wrong word, maybe. Sensitively, sympathetically.*

Because you need to have a sort of rapport with the music you're playing in order to be able to express it.

SN: *You've got to have every emotion in the book, whether it's anger, love, sadness. You are playing your own emotions. And it will be different every day.*

GB: *When I look at a piece with them, I take it phrase by phrase and say: What is this saying? How is it shaped? There are no limits to the answer to the question of what is it saying? I look at the music to release the emotion of a piece, to reveal it first and to allow them to release it.*

✥ LANGUAGE ✥

GB: *It's their personal images; let the person find their own image, no matter how discontinuous, no matter how much there is absence of story or script. As long as it is a script which is vivid to them. I'm always saying that looking at a piece of music is like looking at a piece of sculpture. It is the same piece of sculpture but as you walk around it, it looks different. Colour is of the utmost importance. Because we are intensely visual as animals. When we talk about colour, it is metaphorical in the utmost. On the guitar we have distinct ways of referring to registration on the string, each of which produces a highly characteristic sound. For that we use the word 'colour'. Flutey, or mellow or brassy.*

SN: *Sometimes I make up words. If it's a song or an aria, I make up words to it. Because then it means something. Or I talk about cooking. It's no good cooking unless you can visualise what it will look like on the plate. Roast beef, Yorkshire pud. Fresh vegetables. You make the dish and you've forgotten one thing, the gravy. To me the gravy is the music.*

ET: *I tend to use words like dancing or energetic. And I try to stimulate a response by using colour, in the ambience sense. I say that dynamic is a mood or an atmosphere. For example, if someone is playing Debussy, I will make them go along and look at a lot of Impressionistic paintings to understand that kind of language. I talk about tone colours a lot. Piano actually means nothing; a dynamic marking on paper is an indication of how that piece should sound to the audience.*

SY: *I talk about sound a lot. I use thick or thin; hard or soft, a warm sound. You can tell a lot about someone from their sound. They have to be physically relaxed, and if they believe in a sense of direction, then getting somewhere is what produces the emotion.*

With all the teachers, a combination of technique, a physical relationship to the instrument, and then metaphor or image lead to the point where the performer's contribution makes the difference between 'playing the notes' and 'playing the music'.

It is clear that the teaching process is largely a pragmatic one, not necessarily consciously based on specific theoretical aesthetics, or on convictions about the nature of music as a distinct art form – at least, not on a first level of discussion. Each teacher does, of course, hold explicit or implicit views about this, but these do not seem to enter the conscious teaching process. A level of abstraction is used in the way images and the concept of 'colour' are used. The latter is the most curious, since it is virtually always generic rather than specific, and somehow in the teaching process this appears to convey meaning which links the purely technical (ie, where it is on the guitar) with an expressive result. However, what is 'yellow'? What is 'red'? How does the reference to a colour translate into a sound? Why did none of them use the word 'timbre'?

Just as none of the aestheticians have produced a convincing account of the relationship between emotion and music, so the language of musician/teachers, with decades of experience, appears to be indirect and inadequate, suggestive rather than precise. It does not mean that they are unsuccessful in their teaching; far from it. One could simply assert that there is no vocabulary (words) to apply to performance, and that's why metaphor enters the field. That's why it is always indirect: look at an Impressionist painting and then play Debussy. Feel 'sad' and then play a phrase. Does that mean there is only one way to play 'sad'? Does that mean the phrase itself is sad?

A provisional and provocative answer might be that the best route is for sound to respond to sound. However, while that may be accurate, and seem to offer a relief from the complexities of how to use language about/in relation to music, it is only temporary. What all of the above shows (even proves?) is that emotion/ meaning in relation to the music – at least, in the process of performing it – relies on associative, extrinsic elements, which are then verbalised in a variety of ways.

❧ PROFESSIONAL PERFORMERS ❧

I approached two professional performers, with many years of experience between them. Penelope Cave (PC) is a harpsichordist and teacher. Sir Roger Norrington (RN) is a conductor:

When you are practising/performing, do you ever consciously think about, or 'attach' specific emotions to the music?

PC: *Yes, I certainly do experience specific emotions within the music I play, that appear to me to be intrinsic to the work, rather than something I have inflicted upon it. I probably would be unable to find a piece to which I didn't have an emotional response. However, in describing them I attach language to what the composer makes me feel, so it is reactive rather than proactive if that makes sense? However, I think there might be three levels of perception:*

A completely subconscious knowledge of emotional meaning.

I think this is a gift, because it probably cannot be learnt, but it is something I have always been very certain about and will need to share with hand-movements and dance, or express in words, rather than it be overlooked. There is an innate musical awareness, I feel, that applies particularly to the emotion of 'longing' – the placing of the second note of an upward minor 6th for example, an instinctive rubato, or to a recognition of the numinous.

Pre-reading or anticipating the required emotion of a piece of music by the initial clues, such as title, speed, time-signature, stylistic markings, texture, and often key, to make a Scherzo sound witty, or a March, triumphant, and a Nocturne, dreamy, etc. Couperin helpfully adds comments, to his pièces de clavecin, such as grotesquement for L'Arlequine and thus, seemingly, 'gives permission' for a more exaggerated portrait of this ungainly, yet not unlovable, character. One should not forget that a single work might contain diverse emotions, and even more than one concurrently! This is, of course, a broad-brush starting-point, and an aid to a performance (that might be seen as an actor's artificial adoption of emotion), to which detail is added as better known; the 'triumphant' march might be further categorised as regal, noble, or militant, as it becomes humanised, genuinely propelled by the emotion of pride, or belligerence, perhaps.

Becoming conscious of an over-riding or more deeply-felt emotion, as one learns and performs music (the audience can feed back and enhance an emotional current). An example might be the first fugue in the Bach Toccata in E minor which I started to describe to myself as a rare example of a 'bossy' Subject. I do, deliberately, search for the individual emotions of fugue subjects, because we need to clearly delineate every bit of characterisation, in order for it to hold its own and be recognisable throughout the work. Then there are those pieces which one almost defines by the acute desolation and agony they inspire, such as Louis Couperin's F# minor Pavane.

I asked Sir Roger Norrington the following:

When preparing music for rehearsal, do you think about, take into account, the possible emotional aspects of the music?

In rehearsing – as a conductor – do you convey any/all of these, and if so, in what way?

RN: *Oh yes. I take emotion immediately into account, as the primary driver of the composer and of the performer. I am not attracted to music which does not have an evident emotional cargo. Of course, there are many other issues of primary importance: purpose, structure, attractiveness, rhythmic interest, harmonic subtlety, orchestral colour, and so on. But emotion is the core. The phenomenal challenge for the composer is to handle what must necessarily be an overwhelming emotional reaction to all his surroundings, while having the fantasy, and the technical skill, to create intelligible, compelling, structures. That's why there are so few great ones.*

In the Classic era, where it is actually the central subject matter, the emotion is often joy, the satisfaction of brilliant conversation.

In the nineteenth century things often become much more serious. It is not only Berlioz in the Fantastique who poured out his emotions into a programme. It's difficult not to find programmes in Beethoven 3, 5, or 9; nor in Tchaikovsky, Dvorak, even Brahms Symphonies. And I think it was Walton who said that 'you can't write a big piece like a symphony unless something terrible has happened to you'. At the very end of that century Mahler never wrote a bar that was not emotional, or indeed about him!

In rehearsal I don't spend a lot time discussing these things. Orchestras shrink from overt emotion; they like to reveal it in their playing. I let it become clear from my gesture, and while clarifying points of detail as we proceed. Best conducting is from sharing, not dictating. That sharing is much easier if one conducts from memory, and listens a lot. Some audiences like an elaborate show of emotion from conductors. I prefer more modest means. But the emotion must always be evident.

You conduct orchestras, where there is unison playing. Do they all have to 'feel' the same emotion – or doesn't it matter, as long as the sound is 'right' for you, and is there a sense in which all this is/has to be beyond words?

RN: *More than one composer has explained that music can express things that mere words cannot.*

On the other hand, there is the famous story of the conductor asking for the morning dew at sunrise, and the players replying, 'You mean louder or softer, Maestro?'

With good orchestras I can hear them 'getting it'. No, it doesn't matter if they have their own different interpretations, as long as the music 'speaks'.

Some of our Stuttgart audiences felt they were being directly addressed by the orchestra. Sounds good to me.

CHAPTER FOUR

The Conditions of Performance

Even where writers on music make comparisons with literature and drama; even where they admit that meaning varies from culture to culture, from one period of history to another, and from one musical style to another, there is very little discussion of the social, material medium of performance as a conveyor of meanings.

A series of eight books, with the pre-feminist title, *Man and Music* (in the US it had the more enlightened title, *Music and Society*), aims to 'present music in a broad context of socio-political, economic, intellectual and religious life'. The series is closely linked to the New Musicology, and its project to analyse music in context. Editor Iain Fenlon points out that while compositional techniques, forms and styles are all important, the book is concerned to relate style and changes in style to:

... changes in the function of music itself, which are in turn responses to changes in the structures and needs of society ... religious change, the impact of printing and the growth in influence of the bourgeoisie, all of which are intimately and inextricably related ... [139]

Musical Instruments and their Symbolism in Western Art[140] pioneered 'musical iconology'. Emanuel Winternitz analyses the symbolic function of pictorial structure in delineating the social status of musicians (high or low), and the religious, erotic and political allegories associated with various instruments. Sounds

139   Ed. Iain Fenlon, blurb to *The Renaissance* (Prentice Hall, 1989)
140   Winternitz, Emanuel (Yale University Press, 1979)

have been thought to have meanings in themselves – such as the sexual symbolism carried by wind instruments. A similar strand of analysis is continued in Richard Leppert's *Music and Image*,[141] which focuses on eighteenth-century painting and English domestic music-making.

Winternitz and Leppert's work relate to ideas derived from semiology, developed in the early twentieth century. According to Jonathan Culler,[142] Ferdinand de Saussure argued that:

... language is a system of signs. Noises count as language only when they serve to express or communicate ideas; otherwise they are just noise. And to communicate ideas they must be part of a system of conventions, part of a system of signs.[143]

... the distinction between 'langue' and 'parole' has important consequences for other disciplines besides linguistics, for it is essentially a distinction between institution and event, between the underlying system which makes possible various types of behaviour and actual instances of such behaviour.[144]

'Langue' and 'parole' mirror the two definitions of style in an earlier chapter (ie, dialect and idolect): there is a general cultural style in the early part of the nineteenth century, and there are the specifics of Beethoven's style. The matter of signs and their context has implications for performance:

In all cases where we are dealing with what Saussure calls values, that is to say with the social significance of objects and actions, the subject takes on a crucial role, in that the facts one is seeking to explain come from ... intuitions and judgement. However, once the subject is in place ... firmly established at the centre of the analytical domain, the whole enterprise of the human sciences becomes one of deconstructing the subject, of explaining meanings in terms of

141   CUP, 1993
142   Culler, Jonathan, *Saussure* (Fontana, 1976)
143   Ibid, p19
144   Ibid, p33

systems of convention which escape the subject's conscious grasp. The speaker of a language is not consciously aware of its phonological and grammatical systems in whose terms ... judgements and perceptions will be explained. Nor is the subject necessarily aware of its own psychic economy or of the elaborate system of social norms which govern behaviour.[145]

Though these ideas formed the basis of linguistics, the principles allow for ways to show how a careful analysis of the conditions of musical performance (not just the music itself) can demonstrate the importance of extrinsic factors and how they serve to determine meanings.

Classical music performance works in a way very different from its fellow performance arts – dance and theatre. Compared with theatre, the concert convention tends to be the one-off performance, as opposed to a series of repeated performances (runs), across weeks, months or even years. Music performance is itinerant; rehearsals are often minimal, sometimes just on the afternoon of performance. This practice relies on familiarity with the repertoire, technical competence, and (in England) a reputation for good sight-reading.

Unlike theatre and dance, only soloists, among musicians, learn their music by heart. A production of Hamlet, where the rest of the cast 'read' from scripts, would be considered amateur, or staged in such a hurry that no-one had had time to learn their words. By contrast, audiences are completely accustomed to seeing musicians play from sheet music on stage.

Although – as in the theatre – most musicians are freelance, there are some secure forms of employment, which affect musical style/quality. Chamber groups work together over years, build repertoire and develop their own styles. Large orchestras produce performances from a rehearsed repertoire, with musicians on contract, providing security of employment and income. Concert

---

145   Ibid, p78

staging is cheap and simple: no set, apart from chairs, stands and/ or keyboard. Everyone brings their own clothes and props (instruments). Opera is more like theatre, because rehearsing a dramatic piece involves time, sets, investment and dramatic ensemble co-ordination.

Within the relative simplicity of concert stage presentation, the framing of performance is crucial to what is communicated to the audience. This is not to dismiss the consummate standards of musicianship, or the importance of the music itself. However, the conventions of performance articulate and mediate the music, shaping and, to a greater or lesser extent, framing and 'creating' the over-arching meanings of the event.

The main framing device in chamber music concerts is a disruptive one. A group will come on, bow, smile, not necessarily in a co-ordinated way, then tune, before playing. The tuning has a technical function, of course, but it also functions as a public warm-up. It prepares the musicians to tune to the ambient sound in situ, preparing for performance in the same acoustic. It allows the audience to settle, and listen to the tuning, creating the (upbeat) silence which precedes the first musical sound.

A fundamental difference between theatre and music, is the way in which the 'fourth wall', that invisible division between performers and audience, is negotiated. In music – chamber and orchestral – the fourth wall is constantly disrupted. In orchestras, conductor, first violin, soloists and singers will come on and go off stage at intervals, bowing before and after playing, garnering applause each time. This means there is, periodically, direct contact with the audience – that is, regularly breaching the fourth wall.

By contrast, in theatre, applause is limited to before the interval and at the end of the show. This maintains the continuity of narrative and performance, and fixes the fourth wall as an invisible barrier. Of course, during theatre performances audiences may gasp, laugh, even sometimes briefly applaud something, but the cast always remain within their self-contained world.

Theatre thus carries conscious narrative continuity over a longer time scale than even a fairly lengthy symphony. Concerts have natural 'breaks' between items, since musical continuity only obtains within each composition, not cross-compositionally. This may appear to provide a justification for constantly breaching the fourth wall – but there could be more organic ways of sustaining stage continuity.

With chamber groups, it is not uncommon for the musicians to come onstage, bow, look round the audience, to see who is there, even occasionally smile or nod to someone they know in the front rows. This carries overtones of the school play, in which children cannot separate their role as performers from the need to see where Mummy and Daddy are, and by implication to say, 'Look at me'.

Musicians often leave the stage when they are not playing, or between pieces. A singer might come on to join instrumentalists – more applause to greet him/her, and the same again when s/he exits. Sometimes the whole group will leave – garnering applause each time they leave and return. Sometimes stage hands move music stands and/or chairs. The audience shift in their seats, chat, and then the programme resumes.

It could be argued that this very informality and the constant disruption of the fourth wall is a product of the fragmented nature of the concert repertoire. It could be argued that it gives the audience more chances to feel part of the event – applauding with thanks and pleasure, showing the musicians how satisfying their performances are. It could be argued that such mixing of presentational modes echoes something of the Victorian drawing-room atmosphere, where audience and performers mingled. It could be argued that the gaps between the discrete pieces in each performance allows the audience to relax, chat, comment, gossip, consult their programmes or just gaze vacantly into the air. Interestingly, the modern convention of not applauding between the movements of (say) a symphony, shows some awareness of musical continuity, where the 'silences' are only pauses.

However, the recurrent disruptions of the fourth wall belong more to a polemical than a performative convention. In the polemical convention, contact with the audience is essential, since the speaker(s) are addressing the audience, and thus the fourth wall is a space barrier, rather than a statement about the self-contained onstage performance. This makes the concert format closer to a – non-fiction, as it were – event, with punctuating aesthetic experiences – a hybrid, which at best, can communicate contradictory messages.

Theatrical events are predicated on dramatic irony. Performance is self-contained, independent of the audience, which is collusively eavesdropping. Each party on either side of the invisible wall knows the other party is there, and both parties collude in their knowledge about the 'other'. The stage 'pretends' not to know the audience is there, the audience 'pretends' not to know that the stage knows they are there. It's like the familiar pantomime cry: 'He's behind you'. Dramatic irony is relieved with the structured allowance of applause at the interval and at the end.

Theatre is a 'closed', continuous, aesthetic event. Concerts contain no dramatic irony; each 'side' is constantly acknowledging the existence of the other. This could be argued as a performative honesty. However, the combination of the polemic and the aesthetic, in which the latter is regularly disrupted by the former, denies the theatricality of performance proper. The framing device determines the meaning of the overall event. This is not to devalue the music or the musicians. It is to show that discussions about the 'meaning' in and of the music must take place in relation to the specific conditions of each performance.

J. S. Bach's St Matthew Passion

Bach's cantatas, oratorios and other music, marking moments in the Christian liturgical calendar, included the *St Matthew Passion*, written in 1727, and first performed in Leipzig. It was apparently radical in its mixture of familiar chorales (which its audience joined in singing) and the more original 'theatrical' recitative/aria/arioso forms, which shocked some of its contemporary audience, more used to sacred solemnity.

The piece has come to be accepted as one of the landmarks of the early music revival. Felix Mendelssohn, at the age of twenty, conducted its first revival performance from the piano, in 1829 in Berlin. There was a choir of 158 singers, together with a full-sized orchestra of the day. As the nineteenth century progressed, enthusiasm for Bach's music grew, and the *St Matthew Passion* is regularly scheduled on our concert calendar at Easter.

The popularity of the *St Matthew Passion* in contemporary England demonstrates both a cultural 'fit' and cultural discrepancies. The timing of performances for Easter is suitable, because of the story of the Passion. Easter also may coincide with the Jewish festival of Passover, and the Islamic festival of Ramadan. These different religious festivities can be linked (exact timings vary from year to year) by the Easter weekend, which extends through Good Friday, over to Easter Monday, which is also a secular – bank – (public) holiday.

The following is a comparative analysis of four performances of J.S. Bach's *St Matthew Passion* in the mid 1990s. Each performance is described and analysed for the distinctive elements which create its conditions of performance and thus its dominant meanings.

☙ KING'S COLLEGE, CAMBRIDGE ❧

This performance took place in King's College Chapel,

Cambridge. The printed programme is a veritable work of art, with a beautiful matt black cover, an (unattributed) illustration of the crucifixion on the front and reversed out parts of the musical facsimile on the black end papers. The performance (and further products for sale) are sponsored by some fourteen European organisations – 'Production Partners' – whose names are discreetly tucked inside the cover flap. Tickets cost £50 a head. No gloss spared. Inside, the text is framed by laudatory blurb copy: writing about the 'eternal beauty' of the music, 'a unified, sacred work of art', and then comes the hard sell:

We as producers, stand in awe before this mighty masterpiece of musical, religious and philosophical architecture ... One guarantee for quality is the excellent cast for this Passion. The enthusiastic involvement of our favourite musicians in this project has been the solid foundation on which we have been building. In all our productions it has been a constant challenge to create a refreshing symbiosis between historically informed and state-of-the-art technology performance.

We will prove that High Definition Television, Digital Video Compact Disc and modern theatre technology need not be in contradiction with period authenticity. The essential link is something as simple as 'beauty'.

Blurb writing is never easy. In order to strike a portentous tone, the above prose sometimes reads as if it is a translation from another language. More important, the rationalisation of 'period' performance as congruent with hi-tech is given prominence by the use of capital letters to denote the electronic media. Normally, with a sacred text, only the divine is allowed the honour of capital letters in English. Technology, it seems is Divine, as well as being trade-marked.

There are contradictory messages. First, the assertion that 'beauty' (the aesthetic) is the most important aspect of the performance. Next, a re-arranging of the hierarchy of categories:

in the absence of the Father, the Son, and the Holy Ghost, we have High Definition Television and Digital Video Compact Disc. A typographical coup with the mere flick of upper-case keys, reveals a set of motivations and meanings that are, in the final instance, commercial, and, at the very least, competing with the divine. While not directly spiritual, they might allow many (the buyers of the video) access to a private, leisurely spiritual experience which they can switch on and off at will, at home, at any time. This is a far cry from the convention of live performance as part of a religious service, even one given in a beautiful and famous ecclesiastical setting, such as King's College Chapel.

The contextualization is overwhelmingly secular. While the 'sacred' content is mentioned, the power is in the self-aggrandisement of the 'patrons': self-congratulatory, for landing the best professionals, high prices for the tickets, countering the sacred convention of a church open to all. The question is whether the commercial secularity either overwhelms the 'spiritual' message, or if, at the very least, it is at odds with it. If the latter, the message received by the audience is more likely to reinforce their privilege, rather than the more spiritual message of the story.

THE ROYAL FESTIVAL HALL, LONDON

The performance on Palm Sunday, at the Royal Festival Hall, reverses some of the above features. Whereas at King's there is a period baroque orchestra, with Roy Goodman conducting from the first violin, here both choir and orchestra are unashamedly modern. In the bowl of the auditorium is a choir of some 300 voices. Two adult choirs are arranged male/female, not according to 'voice', and in the centre, a *ripieno* school choir, in white shirts, contrasts with the all black outfits of the adults.

The members of the orchestra wander on and tune to the ambient A from the oboes, in a cacophony of sound, just as they would for a conventional concert. Individual instrumentalists warm up by going over some of their difficult passages. Then, over the tannoy, comes a disembodied male voice (whose God?) requesting that, because of the nature of the work, there should be no applause before, during or after the performance. An audience arriving in the usual way for a concert is being asked to ignore a concert convention – as if they might be in church.

Conductor David Willcocks enters with the soloists: the men in grey pinstripe trousers, black morning coats, and dark waistcoats. The women wear evening concert dress, one in dark velvet, with low-cut front and back, the other in slimline black and white glitter, as if dressed for a formal social occasion. Choir and orchestra wear more sober, smart casual variants on the black colour code.

The choir and all but one of the soloists use black folders for their music. The one with a different colour is very noticeable. The soloists stand at the front of the stage; some adopt an impersonal, self-effacing mien when they are not singing; one or two allow their eyes to scan the audience. The soloists do not join in either choruses or chorales. Throughout the performance, the huge choir rises and sits as one – doubtless carefully choreographed and rehearsed.

The English text is articulated with great clarity, although inevitably, as in any sung performance, large chunks of it are swallowed up in the overall acoustic. The words are printed in the programme, which some of the audience follow, while others do so with pocket scores. This means that some of the audience read and hear, but don't watch, the performance.

Obediently, there is no applause, and, at the interval, a respectful hush mixes gently with the sounds of members of the audience leaving their seats – something they would not do *en masse* in the middle of a church service. Interestingly, the performance takes up a large part of the day, with facilities laid on for people to eat their 'picnic' lunches, lending the event an air of pilgrimage – of a very comfortable (if it dare be said) middle-class cultural experience.

As with the King's performance, there are conflicts between the spiritual and the secular. It could be said that once the secularity of the framing is set aside – ie, when the audience is seated – a 'modernised' presentation of the baroque piece may yield some emotional and/or spiritual appreciation. However, the fact that there are visible numbers of people following the music from their own copies, adds a pedagogic air to the procedure. Do they 'feel' as if they are participating? Are they, teacher-like, checking to see there are no mistakes? A number of possible 'meanings' are available, which determine the audience's experience, conscious or not. Despite the request not to applaud, the sense/meaning is of a concert, not a liturgical performance: a secular event, which conflicts with the internal message of the words/music.

ST JOHN'S, SMITH SQUARE

The performance at St John's, Smith Square, with conductor David Chernaik, is more informal than the other two. As at the Festival Hall, the orchestra consists of modern instruments, with a smaller choir of about forty people.

Four soloists stand at the front, and one joins in singing the chorales (standard nineteenth-century practice). Jesus and the Evangelist/narrator are placed among the orchestra, and therefore – from the audience's point of view – appear and disappear, as they stand and sit, unlike the other soloists, who are visible throughout. The varied casual staging might have been deliberate, or simply have been due to the fact that there was no room for all the soloists at the front of the stage.

The choir is onstage as the audience filters in. Most of the choir wear black, with a scattering of coloured shirts – purple, blue, turquoise and red. Soloists and conductor come on to applause, and bow. The men wear dinner jackets and bow ties, the women are in black and white glitter, less elaborate than the Festival Hall women soloists. David Chernaik, the conductor, sports a turquoise silk shirt, and no jacket.

The prologue is followed by applause and a hiatus, during which the conductor looks towards the other end of the auditorium. Just as the pause is on the brink of embarrassment, the conductor turns back and raises his baton. Jesus and the Evangelist stand up from among the orchestra, and it appears that the conductor has been waiting for latecomers to take their seats. The disruption of both atmosphere and musical continuity is disconcerting.

No-one onstage has their music in folders. The text is sung in the original German, unlike the Festival Hall English. The choir launches into the chorales with the feeling of a church choir leading the congregation. However, that would have been impossible, since the choir is singing in German and the text in the programme is in English.

The framing is full of difference/contradictions. Somewhat scrappy staging, modern instruments, yet with the text in the original German. The atmosphere is concert, rather than church-like. It could be argued that this kind of hybrid is appropriate to the modern moment. However, it feels more as if someone (the conductor?) has not made a clear decision as to whether this is a secular experience, or a musical continuum with spiritual impact.

ꙮ BBC 2 ꙮ

On the afternoon of Good Friday there is a broadcast on BBC2 TV of the *Passion*, billed as a 'dramatised' production, and described in the *Radio Times* as 'a music drama recorded specially for TV (a video and CD will be released soon)'. The event was first performed – with a live audience – the previous year at Holy Trinity Church, Chelsea. It is directed by Jonathan Miller, writer and opera producer, and staged in the round (no audience), with two young choirs and period instruments. The TV performance was recorded in St George's Church, Tufnell Park, in North London, also without an audience. Baroque oboist Paul Goodwin conducts what the *Radio Times* describes as the 'Passion Band', a nomenclature which immediately implies that everyone is fused with the 'content' of the story.

As the prologue sounds, there is a series of stills of period instruments. The camera angles consist of middle- to close-up shots of players and singers, with some middle-distance shots. At no moment do we have any idea where we are: it could be a church, a theatre, a concert hall, a large room. Such 'setting' as we can see is minimal and suggestive: a bare wooden table, wooden chairs and a wooden floor; lighting that suggests the yellows and browns of Dutch portrait painting. Period (and reconstruction period) instruments, small forces, recorders as well as flutes, all combine the old (past) with the modern (present state of the art – technology). Bread and wine on the table are picked up by Jesus, but not handed round.

The ensemble wears variants on casual, 1990s clothes: jeans, checked shirts, sweaters, polo necks, loose scarves – creating the feeling that we are eavesdropping on a rehearsal.

Some instrumentalists play from music, some play from memory. There is, however, nothing casual about the attitude to performance, instrumental and vocal. At all times (except for one glimpse of an oboist in the background scratching her nose) when they are not playing, instrumentalists and singers look at, and listen to, the singers, just as actors and actresses listen to each other onstage. If the dramatic moment demands it, singers give attention to the Evangelist. The 'cast' is united in the single performance, much in the way that the cast of a play has to be,

The intensity of the event is enhanced by the camera, which moves unobtrusively among players and singers, so that the viewer is almost part of the ensemble. There is a fourth wall here, but it is not that of live performance: it is an absolute technological divide, between performers and the distanced invisible audience, which cannot be breached.

Paradoxically, the combination of absolute distance and 'internal' intimacy makes the fourth wall – virtually – disappear. Rather than disrupting the event, the 'barrier' of the wall is annihilated, as we are taken into the middle of the action. Especially effective are the face-to-face duo moments between solo singers and their obbligato instruments, as if we, the distanced audience, are eavesdropping on private moments.

The conventions of dramatic performance dominate. The narrator/Evangelist controls the action, paralleling the liturgical practice where a 'priest' leads a service, guiding fellow-celebrants and congregation through the ritual. Here the Evangelist-narrator is an intermediary between all the elements, including the distanced audience; now singing direct to camera (us), now prompting dramatic action by addressing Jesus or others in the 'cast'.

The close-up intimacy gradually reveals the fact that the orchestra is almost entirely female. There is a line in the *Passion* referring to the 'many women' who followed Jesus, and by subtle implication (conscious or not), this is mirrored in the instrumental casting. The story of Jesus being followed by women is reflected by Jesus (the singer) being followed, supported, led by women (instrumentalists, band, and soloists). The same pattern is repeated at the 'external' work-force level, where the conductor (male) is in charge of, and the final point of reference for, a predominantly female music-population. Jesus and conductor take on similar leadership roles. Thus, while we have greater (and radical) presence of women in the musical work-force, men are still in charge.

Conclusion: Meaning and the Conditions of Performance

The comparative analysis of four performances of the same piece of music demonstrates how their presentation and framing devices generate and determine different meanings, which affect the way in which the so-called 'pure' musical elements might be received.

This directly affects the over-arching meanings of the musical event, highlighted, in this instance, by the fact that there is a narrative (sung words) which carry a specific, spiritual message. One might begin by assuming that the same 'message' is conveyed through the music, no matter where and how it is performed. However, this is not the case. The conditions of performance determine the meanings, spiritual and secular.

The King's College performance was framed and overlaid with the commercial and social messages, lending the *Passion* a strongly commodified impact, despite the period orchestra, and historically informed performances. One could argue that any spiritual message was thus very much less important than the shop-front of an expensive, privileged occasion for the audience.

The Festival Hall performance sought to mirror liturgical and ecclesiastical framings: no applause, a 'pilgrimage' event over a whole day. However, the musical forces deployed were closer to nineteenth than eighteenth-century practice. An attempt at authentic framing is countered by the inauthentic presentation of the actual music. The sense of a secular day out with picnic is strongest, rather than any sense of commitment to a devotional occasion.

The informal, not to say scrappy, presentation at St John's, Smith Square, with uncertain inner pacing, was, despite being in a former church, scarcely different from any other concert. It harnessed neither the highest features of theatrical presentation, nor the ritualised formality of the liturgy. Consequently, any spiritual satisfaction would have come from a pre-existing familiarity with the work. Any spiritual meaning associated with the narrative, would have come from outside the concert hall, since it had hardly been 'produced' within it.

Ironically, it is the most technologically intensive performance by the BBC which came closest to conveying both the historical authenticity of instruments and styles of performance, with a 'hot line' to the spiritual message. This event harnessed the sophistication and formality of high-quality concert expertise to render an appearance of serious spiritual reinforcement. A case of having one's secular cake and spiritually eating it. This came about as a result of a series of paradoxes. The technology managed to breach the fourth wall (recording and screen) by creating an intimacy with individual clusters of audience (at home), forming a distanced – and serially, private – congregation.

By creating a seamless, uninterrupted theatrical production, without applause (ie, as in church), and by eschewing the Victorian formalities of dinner jackets and evening dress, the music was communicated with fewer explicit cultural associations to get in the way.

Historically informed instruments and performance provided access to one form of authenticity – with contemporary theatrical and technological means unashamedly demonstrating historical distance. Taking the spiritual message into the audience's homes, via the TV screen, allowed for a direct intimacy which echoed the significance of the spiritual message conveyed as part of an ecclesiastical service. Here, while the congregation is physically atomised (separated), the focused intensity of the form and its technical medium create a closer bond between audient(s), performers and the music itself. So, ironically, the very physical and technological distance between performers and audience actually comes closest – if it can be put in this way – to the original, devotional message.

PART TWO

CHAPTER FIVE

Idiomatic Music 1

Scholarship and Authenticity

A late developer among the humanities, musical scholarship provides one of the last strongholds of respectability for the editor.[146]

Musical scholarship has been responsible for reviving lost and/or forgotten music, and this has enabled performances, established repertoire, and expanded the aural landscape. Especially important was the publication of editions of music in Germany, which helped to lay the foundations of today's musical canon. Philip Brett comments on the importance of editions of Bach, Handel, Palestrina and Beethoven, which appeared from the 1850s onwards:

This was the first serious and systematic attempt to establish the works of musical authors in a canonic way: the editions of Mendelssohn, Mozart, Chopin, Schumann and others that quickly followed, indicate its success. It had the incidental effect, one might say, of canonising the German tradition to which these composers belonged, either in fact or by adoption.[147]

There are some parallels between literary and musical scholarship. For example, the first complete edition of seventeenth-century John Donne's poetry[148] included poems of doubtful

146   Brett, Philip, 'Text. Context and the Early Music Editor', in *Authenticity and Early Music* ed. Nicholas Kenyon (OUP, 1988), p83
147   Ibid, p86
148   *The Complete English Poems*, ed. A.J. Smith (Penguin, 1971)

authorship (where circumstantial and stylistic evidence supported attribution), textual selection based on comparisons of different sources, and some modernised spellings and punctuation. Notes provided variant readings, and explanations of archaic, or metaphorically complex, language. The editor's project was similar to that of a music editor – 'to make an old and difficult author as intelligible as is now possible to readers of today'.[149]

Musical scholarship also reveals the original, 'authentic', 'ur' copy/record. The equivalent of modernised spelling lies in post-nineteenth-century editing conventions: updating note values (ie, not using breves), performer-guidance (some might say performer-proof) markings: dynamics, expression marks, metronome tempi. Such additions are analogous to stage directions in a written dramatic text. In both cases, the 'markings' appear to 'instruct' the performance, ie, what happens when the music is lifted off the page.

When the indications are instrument-specific – ie, bow-strokes, articulation – these editorial additions lead to (or reinforce) the idea that any given piece of music 'fits', is only suited to, the instrument (or voice) for which it is, or may be, designated. In other words, it will be considered 'idiomatic'.

The Harvard New Dictionary of Music offers a succinct definition of the idiomatic:

Of a musical work, exploiting the particular capabilities of the instrument or voice for which it is intended ... [150]

The New Grove has no specific entry for 'idiomatic'; it presents the concept as an extension of style:

It was ... in the late Renaissance and early Baroque that theoretical discussion of style became an important area of literary production;

---

149   Ibid, p15
150   *The New Harvard Dictionary of Music,* ed. Don Randel (Harvard University Press, 1986)

indeed the word 'style' enters the vocabulary of musical commentary at this time.

> *The resources of performance are important formative influences on style ... Characteristic sounds are a direct element of style, while the techniques of performing on specific resources, with attendant idiomatic proclivities and possibilities, influence melody, rhythm and texture ... Voices are good at sustained conjunct music, while instruments are suited to agility and disjunction. The violin has a capacity for wide-ranging melody, as Corelli exploited, and very high tessitura as Romantic composers found.*[151]

It sounds from this as though there are correlations between certain forms of expression, and the means (voices and/or instruments) whereby they are communicated. That is not the case. Fifteenth- and sixteenth-century instrumental monody often only indicated 'soprano' or 'prima parte'. A title page might say the music is for 'ogni sorti di stromenti' (different kinds of instruments) and the music itself would have been transposed (even at sight) if necessary.

In early seventeenth-century music, the burgeoning instrumental sonata did not always distinguish between string and wind, giving the option of either. By the early eighteenth century, it was still customary to list the various instruments on which the music could be played. It was common practice to transpose up a minor or major third, moving from baroque flute or violin to recorder, for example, or at the octave for string instruments. This means it was taken for granted that sonorities/ timbres could vary for the same piece of music. Indeed, the French viol player and composer, Marin Marais, even commented in 1689 that ' ... *nowadays in France everyone transposes so easily by tones and semi-tones.*'[152]

---

151   *New Grove Dictionary of Music and Musicians* ed. Stanley Sadie, Vol 18 (OUP, 1980), p8

152   *Marin Marais Translated* Ian Gammie (Corda Music, 1989)

All this implies a different approach from today's notions of 'reading'. For musicians nurtured on the idea that there is an inexorable 'fit' between instrument and music, and the idea that one only plays a single instrument, it appears to be an outdated practice. However, as Hans Keller points out, there was still some flexibility into the twentieth century:

> *Until, and indeed slightly beyond, the first quarter of this century, a good violinist automatically was a viola player at the same time; the fact was not worth mentioning.*[153]

During the eighteenth century, along with the (unsuccessful) attempts to codify musical affect, a similar move to 'fix' the idiomatic began to emerge. Composers who specifically designated music for the violin, incorporated solo virtuosic elements, such as double and triple stopping, arpeggiated moto-perpetuo movements – most familiar through work such as Corelli's Opus V, first published in 1700.[154] This was enormously popular; it was also 'arranged' for a variety of instruments, including bass viol, as concerti grossi (by Geminiani), and, in 1702, for the solo baroque recorder.

Two of the sonatas (C and F major) were published in 1707 as anonymous arrangements for recorder, in the original keys, with the slow movements decorated, and with broken chord figuration for the chordal passages. The publication, by Walsh, Hare and Randall, was advertised as 'illustrated throughout with proper Graces, by an eminent Master'.[155] Such 'Graces' constituted written improvisation for the treble line in the slow movements, and the figured bass line was left to the interpretation of the individual performer.

The bass line in a 1743 edition of trio sonatas by Giuseppe San Martini has stems in two directions, providing a simplified line

153   Keller, Hans, *Criticism* (Faber, 1987), p17
154   *Sonate a Violino o Cimbalo* Opera Quinta (1700). (Facsimile, SPES, 1979)
155   *Sonata in C Major, Opus 5, No 3* ed. D. Lasocki (Musica Rara, 1973)

for the string bass player, and a fully arpeggiated line for the keyboard player to realise.[156]

Telemann's 'Getreue Musik-Meister' (1728) has a number of pieces preceded by three clefs, with three different key signatures, listed 'Flauti dolci, ò à Flauti traversi ò à Viole da gamba'.[157]

You pick your instrument, and read the notes exactly where they are on the stave – according to the clef.

This practice is in a direct line from the Renaissance use of 'chiavetti', 'little keys' used for higher voices, implying transposition – in other words, pitch (like instrumentation) is not an absolute.

Telemann's Getreue Musik-Meister includes a sonata for 'Dessus de viole', notated in alto rather than treble clef, which becomes playable on a string bass or a tenor viol.[158]

---

156   *XII Sonate a due Violini e Violoncello. E Cembalo, so piace* Op 3, No 11, third movement (Walsh, 1743)
157   *Der Getreue Musik-Meister* Telemann (1728), p12
158   Ibid, p97

In French music, recorder, violin, transverse flute and oboe could be dovetailed. All these utilised French violin clef, G1: G on the bottom line reads the same as if it were an F4 bass clef. Hotteterre, in his *L'Art de Preluder sur la Flûte Traversiere, sur la Flûte a bec, sur le Haubois et autres Instrumens de Dessus* (1719) remarks that while G1 and G2 are in use, G1 is the more common and more convenient, since it obviates the need to add ledger lines above the stave – especially for high notes on the recorder. His treatise[159] (for flute, recorder and oboe, and probably written during the 1690s) gives both flute and recorder the G1 (ie, French) clef.

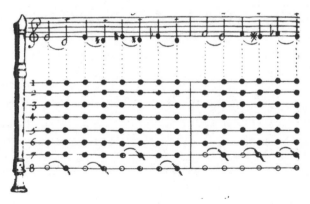

Clef mobility and ways of reading ('interpreting' notation) show that staves – lines and spaces – are fluid, rather than having fixed meanings. The idea of fluidity may even have encouraged a graphic playfulness. Referencing Jonathan Swift's satirical novel,

159   Hotteterre le Romain, *Principes de la Flute Traversiere, ou flute d'Allemagne. De la flute a bec ou Flute douce, et du Haut-Bois* (Etienne Roger, 1728. First published 1707)

Gulliver's Travels, Telemann writes a 'Lilliputsche Chaconne', with tiny fast notes and a 'Brobdingnagische Gigue' with white breves and semi-breves.[160]

The act of 'reading', then, for the eighteenth-century musician (professional or amateur), was far more open-ended than our post-nineteenth-century Pavlovian-reflex expectations, where each musical sign (in non-aleatoric music, anyway) can have only one physical and sonic correlate. In a culture where reading involves choices of instrument and tessitura (interpretation, sonority and transposition), stave and clef are indicators, rather than fixed signs. It is the performer's choice, not the composer or the scribe's, about what instruments are played. The concept of the fixed 'idiomatic' has no place here. Neither has the notion of composer 'intention'.

Editing

Twentieth-century editions of early music combined the predilections of individual editors with their current state of musicological knowledge and performance practice. The difference between editions by Raymond Leppard and Carl Dolmetsch, and those in the more knowledgeable climate of the 1980s and 1990s, demonstrates this.

160 *Der Getreue Musik-Meister,* pp32, 36

Carl Dolmetsch's 'Unaccompanied Sonata for Treble Recorder'[161] has no composer attribution, or information about the original publication. It is by Bach, but there is no BWV number or any source. The text is dotted with slurs, staccato, breath and metronome markings, dynamics and ornaments, none of which are in the original. The customer (performer) is buying a copy of Carl Dolmetsch's notated 'performance', with no sign of where this differs from the original.

4. BOURREE ANGLAISE

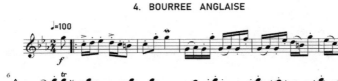

By contrast, the Schott edition of the same sonata in 1983, edited by Paul Zweers, gives us source, BWV 1013, the original key (a minor, transposed up to c minor for the recorder) and tells us exactly where there is (minimal) editorial presence.[162]

161   'Sonata', *J.S. Bach, arr. and edited from the sonata for solo Flute* by Carl Dolmetsch (Universal, 1957)

162   *Partita* J.S. Bach, BWV 1013. Ed. Paul Zweers (Schott, 1983)

Leppard's graphic and elaborate realisations of figured bass in the 1970s is both his 'edition', and 'interpretation' – ie, possibly (probably?) as he played it himself. However, in the example below, there is also an unmeasured grouping of notes, indicating an arpeggiated style, without specifying rhythm – visually more 'open' than a rhythmically precise notation would have been, and thus, curiously, both over-realised and possibly closer to its original performance practice.[163]

Given that there were didactic elements in eighteenth-century music by Hotteterre, Marais and Telemann, one could argue that these modern 'over'-editors were interpreting the spirit of the original, in providing their own performance-based gloss on the music – another form of authenticity.

---

163   Cavalli, arr. Raymond Leppard

Since then there has been a trend for 'clean', unedited, editions, presupposing more knowledgeable performers. Added material can include critical commentaries, concordances, and editorial suggestions in brackets for performance. There has also been a trend towards facsimile publishing – photocopying the original/ur publication, with little or no editorial matter.[164] The conservatoire library in Basel photocopied all five part-books of Marais' volumes of *Pièces de Viole*.[165] In the third volume, Marais states that the pieces 'se peuvent jouer sur plusieurs instruments, comme, l'orgue, le clavesin, le violin, le dessus de viole, le theorbe, la guitarre, la flutte traversiere, la flutte a bec et le hautbois' – and the kitchen sink, one is tempted to add. So much for the idiomatic!

For today's performer, these 'modern' facsimiles are a mixed blessing. Some have the look of an art-book, with quality paper, subtle-colour card covers, and modern title and copyright pages. They provide the 'feel' and sense of getting close to the authentic, the real thing, a reproduction of the same music someone held in past centuries. However, some of these are hard to play from, with spines which make it hard to hold the books open on a stand. The wear and tear that any piece of music gets in rehearsal and performance, may feel more damaging when a book is a pleasure to hold.

Forqueray's pieces for viola da gamba[166] state that they can be played on the pardessus (the smallest member of the viola da gamba family) as well as the bass. They would have to undergo some adaptation ('arrangement') in order to be transferred from the 7-string bass to the 6- or 5-string pardessus. Reputedly, Forqueray himself played contemporary virtuosic Italian violin music on the viol (though we do not know what size). The visual density suggests intensity and excitement, with notation and fingering (original)[167] so black on the page that one would have to

---

164   Publishers such as Minkoff, Fuzeau, Broude Brothers and SPES
165   Published by Rudy Ebner (Facsimile, Basel, n.d.)
166   *Pieces de viole* par M. Forqueray le pere, Paris, 1747 (Facsimile, Minkoff, 1976)
167   Eg, in 'Jupiter'

write the music out for greater clarity and more user-friendly spacing.

As in the earlier Telemann examples, there is visual and musically suggestive pleasure from the 'look' of a facsimile. Marais' 3rd book of *Pièces de Viole*[168] beams the semi-quavers in a fluent, wavy line, invoking the idea of a flowing bow stroke.

Removing barlines from editions of fifteenth-century instrumental polyphony would mean having to find pulse stresses within rhythmically flexible lines, rather than have them dictated by the 'downbeat' stress of barlines. Concepts of syncopation, 'on' and 'off' the beat, are based on the idea of a fixed rhythm, rather than the idea of shifting stresses, and the alternation of duple and triple rhythms.

For today's performer, this presupposes a profound involvement with period repertoires, and wanting to learn other ways of reading.

---

168   *Troisième Livre de Pièces de Viole* Marin Marais, 1711 (Facsimile, Rudy Ebner, Basel, nd)

What was once the province of the outré enthusiast (Dolmetsch et al) has become the staple of a specialist area of the profession and is understood more widely by amateurs and audiences. What began as genuinely enlightening and necessary scholarship – via Leppard, and the invaluable early work in the compendious series Musica Britannica, can now be seen as something that needs to be stripped away from musical presentation, and earlier editorial decisions, which now get in the way of increasingly experienced performers.

CHAPTER SIX

Idiomatic Music 2

Women and the High Viol

IN 1722, JOHN ESSEX offered this advice to young wives:

The Harpsichord, Spinet, Lute and Base Violin are Instruments most agreeable to the Ladies: there are some others that really are unbecoming the Fair sex; as the Flute, Violin and Hautboy; the last of which is too Manlike and would look indecent in a Woman's Mouth; and the Flute is very improper, as taking away too much of the Juices, which are otherwise more necessarily employed, to promote the Appetite and assist Digestion.[169]

This discriminatory attitude towards women (and instruments) ironically provides a useful back-to-front way to use the concept of idiomatic music (ie, the putative 'fit' between music and instrument) to discuss the relationship between gender and music. This is illustrated by the relationship between women and the high viol.

By the twentieth century, the bass viola da gamba was well-nigh obsolete; lying unused, or with new fingerboards, a neck and four strings instead of six or seven – converted to cello-dom. Not surprisingly, cellists were among the first to develop an interest in reviving the gamba and its repertoire. Paul Grummer's tutor for viola da gamba,[170] is written for cellists, deploying their familiar

169   Quoted in Leppert, Richard, 'Music, domestic life and cultural chauvinism', in *Music and Society,* eds. Richard Leppert and Susan McClary (CUP, 1990) p85
170   *Viola da Gamba Schule,* (Anton J. Benjamin, 1928)

bass and tenor clefs, as against the period use of bass and alto clefs. Grummer also uses the tenor clef for studies and exercises, as well as pieces from Simpson's *The Division-Viol*[171] published with bass and alto clefs.

Rediscovering the 6- and 7-string bass gamba, with its repertoire, revealed an extensive musical literature. While there is solo and obbligato music by the German/English composers (Handel, Finger, Abel, J.S. and later C. Ph. E. Bach), the most substantive repertoire is French, with the first known publications from the DuBuisson family during the 1660s. The modern editor of one of the collections notes that solo lute music:

... *significantly influenced the development of work for unaccompanied viol, for the technical capabilities of the two instruments are very similar. In fact, many of the earliest French viol players were also lutenists.*[172]

Further collections were by Le Sieur de Machy in 1685,[173] and the first of Marin Marais' five volumes of *Pièces de Viole*, in 1686. In 1687, Jean Rousseau published his *Traite de la viole*, the first French treatise of its kind.

Already in the sixteenth century, there were nascent examples of solo bass gamba music. The 'viola bastarda' was an elaborated bass line, plundering a piece's harmonic structure, roaming and swooping through other musical lines. Surviving treatises and collections codify what was essentially an extension of improvisation, or the art of playing divisions, which composers, from Ganassi (1535)[174] through to Simpson (1659), thought the mark of the true musician.

The treble viol (in d) was also starting to be considered as a solo instrument. Ganassi declares that while the bass is the most

---

171   Simpson, Christopher, *The Division Viol* 1667 (Facsimile, Curwen, n.d.)
172   Coeyman, 1980
173   *Pieces de Viole,* ed. D. Beecher & B. Gillingham (Dovehouse, 1982)
174   *Regola Rubertina* 1542-3, trans Hildemarie Peter (Robert Lienau, 1972)

important voice, due notice should be given to the soprano in d. Diego Ortiz[175] includes examples of elaborate divisions for treble, among a larger number for the bass. Ian Woodfield[176] notes that as the century progressed, 'the small treble viol (d-tuned) begins to appear more frequently'.

There is some evidence for the presence of the treble viol as a solo instrument in England in an anonymous Jacobean ground and divisions in *Musica Britannica*,[177] along with more extensive division writing for treble and bass viols by Christopher Simpson in the second half of the seventeenth century. However, England did not develop a solo high viol repertoire, perhaps because the viol consort was a more dominating feature of the English court and aristocracy.

The treble is the highest consort voice, although there is speculation that at times it might have been substituted by violins. The 'modernist' music of Jenkins, Lawes and Purcell, where the music ranges above the frets on the treble viol, raises the question of whether such music is better 'suited' to violins – though it could still be played on the treble viol. We are back in the thick of the idiomatic debate, demonstrating that the reclamation and attribution of repertoire is no simple matter. Peter Holman[178] has distilled some of these issues in scholarly detail, although his vested interest is strongly in favour of the violin over the viol.

In France and Germany the emergence of a solo treble viol repertoire may have been connected with those countries' very lack of a viol consort tradition. In Germany, Telemann specified the viol (bass and treble) in about fifty instrumental compositions.[179] Of these, Kinney identified nine trio sonatas which are designated

---

175   *Tratado de Glosas* 1553 (Facsimile, SPES, 1984)

176   Woodfield, Ian, *The Early History of the Viol* (CUP, 1988)

177   Vol 9

178   Holman, Peter, 'The English Royal Violin Consort in the sixteenth century', (*Proceedings of the RMA*, Vol 109, 1982-3)

179   Kinney, Gordon J., 'Telemann's use of the viol as a solo or concertante instrument' (*Journal*, VdGSA. Vol XV11, 1980)

for recorder/oboe and treble viol. In French music there is a considerable body of music designated for the high viol. Adrian Rose[180] draws attention to the presence of the treble viol in a substantial body of French sacred vocal music, in which it is used in counterpoint with the voice, or as a solo ritornello instrument.

Marc-Antoine Charpentier's opera, *Les Arts Florissants* calls for two treble viols. His *Premiere Lecon du Vendredy Saint* of 1670 features solo treble viol, as do the motets of Henri Dumont (1681), and 'a little-known collection by Marc-Antoine Lebeque (1631-1702) which incorporates a sizeable quantity of writing for treble and bass viols ... '[181] Marais uses the generic 'Dessus de violes' in his 1692 publication, *Pieces en trio pour les Flutes, Violons et dessus de Violes*, and later, Hotteterre and Boismortier also include the high viol as one of the treble options in soloistic chamber music.

The first publication explicitly designating the treble viol (dessus de viole) as a 'concertante' instrument appears to be *Trois Suites de pièces a Deux Violles,* by M. Heudelinne, in 1701. The title page adds: 'Qui se peuvent jouer sur le Clavessin & sur le Violon', and in his 'Avertissement', Heudelinne states:

Personne n'ayant encore donne des Pièces pour le Dessus & la basse de Violle ensemble, j'ose esperer que ce Livre, comme le premier, sera de quelque utilite ... [182]

During the late seventeenth and early eighteenth centuries violin music writing became more virtuosic (idiomatic?), exploiting the instrument's technical possibilities: chordal and double stopping, and also coincided with an increase in the upward range of other melody instruments. This probably contributed to the appearance of the 6-string pardessus de viole, tuned a fourth higher than the dessus (the treble), and making it <u>unnecessary to</u> play above the frets of the latter for music that

180   Rose, Adrian P., 'Marc-Antoine Charpentier's *Premier lecon du Vendredy Saint* -an important source of music for solo treble viol' (*Chelys* Vol 13, 1984)
181   Ibid
182   Atelier Philidor, 2015

went up to high d. A pardessus made by Colichon is recorded in 1690. The earliest source of solo music for the 'pardessus de viole' is a collection by Thomas Marc (1724), designated for 'Dessus et de pardessus de Viole'.[183] The original music contains fingering which works for the treble, using notes above the frets.

Publications for the pardessus continued to appear until the late 1760s, and Robert Green speculates that the appearance of the 5-string pardessus around 1740 'seems to have been a symptom of ... (a) growing trend to identify the instrument with the violin'.[184] The tuning of the 5-string exemplifies this overlap. Whereas the 6-string is congruent with other viol tunings – fourths, with a third in the middle, the 5-string consists of fifths and fourths. Green points out that a 'large majority' suggest the pardessus as an alternative to the violin in music published between 1750-1770.[185]

The earliest collection of music designated for 5-string pardessus is by Barthélemy de Caix, published in 1748,[186] and there are ninety publications which mention the pardessus as the primary or alternative instrument on the title page. Green and Rose single out Charles Dolle as possibly the most significant composer for the instrument. Dolle's first collection of solos and duos for pardessus appeared in 1737, and in the same year he published a book of trio sonatas for violins. Dolle designates both the 5- and 6-string pardessus, and Rose suggests that for him 'the pardessus de viole had as much aesthetic merit as did the basse de viole'.[187]

The title page of Forqueray's *Pièces de Viole* (1747) says: 'ces pièces peuvent se jouer sur le Pardessus de Viole'. Hazelle

183   Rose, Adrian, 'Music for the dessus and pardessus de violes, published in France ca. 1650-1770' *Journal* VdGSA, Vol XV1, 1979)

184   Green, Robert A., 'The pardessus de viole and its literature' (*Early Music*, July, 1982)

185   Ibid

186   Green, ibid

187   Rose, Adrian, 'Another collection of pieces by Charles Dolle' (*Chelys* Vol 11, 1982)

Miloradovitch quotes remarks by Daquin and Le Blanc on Forqueray's virtuosic performance of violin music on the viol (not clear what size).[188] She concludes 'that violin sonatas were often played on the bass viol in the eighteenth century'.

She describes a volume of pieces by Corelli, transcribed for 5-string pardessus in 1759 by one Mr de Villeneuve. Miloradovitch concludes, from a manuscript owned by an anonymous figure in Geneva, that 'violin music was commonly played on the five-string pardessus'.

In many of the string treatises, the two families of instruments – viol and violin – (or some of their characteristics) are compared. Hubert le Blanc's *Defense de la Basse de Viole contre les entreprises du violin et les pretentions du violoncello* (1740) is an elegant, allegorical, literary and literal defence of everything about the viol, as against the incursion of the violin – as he saw it. Other treatises discuss comparative bow holds and bowing styles, the function of frets, sound quality (timbre).

As the professionalisation of the violin took off, the high viol increasingly came to be associated with 'cultivated' amateurs and aristocrats – and women, in particular. Writing about the pardessus, Green claims that:

The accumulated evidence suggests that during the early period of the instrument's use – 1720-1740 – it was favoured by a relatively small group of cultivated and accomplished amateurs and professionals. The 5-string instrument developed about 1740 was, after an early period of exploitation by this group, relegated to young ladies and amateurs who could not or would not master (sic) the violin.[189]

The idea that the instrument was 'relegated' to female amateurs, who may have been performing music simpler than that provided

188   Miloradovitch, Hazelle, 'Eighteenth-century manuscript transcriptions for viol of music by Corelli and Marais' (*Chelys* Vol 12, 1983)
189   Green, ibid, 1982

for the violin, is at odds with Miloradovitch's conclusions that virtuosic violin music was often played on the pardessus. It is thus possible that female amateurs preferred playing the pardessus and may even have played virtuosic violin music on it. However, despite the success of one Mme Levi in twelve performances at the Concert Spiritual in 1745, the association of the pardessus with amateurs and young ladies doubtless contributed to the idea that the instrument was not to be taken too seriously.

There is a dynamic which music shares with activities such as embroidery: largely undertaken by women, undervalued and confined to amateur status. In the case of the high viols, surviving iconographical evidence shows a number of drawings and paintings where small viols are played by women – decorously enough to satisfy John Essex's earlier strictures. This, together with the above-mentioned research, suggests that some of these women may well have been (if amateur) virtuosic musicians. However, it took a long time before women were able to train alongside men:

... during most of the 15th and early 16th centuries women had virtually no access to the two kinds of training that constituted the principal means of acquiring a thorough music education: study at a cathedral school or apprenticeship to a master player ... principal music professions (were) closed to them; only those persons who had the opportunity for extensive theoretical training had much hope of mastering the complicated polyphonic style that then prevailed.[190]

Women singers gradually began to be accepted as public performers, especially at the northern Italian courts, such as Ferrara and Mantua. Of the very few women composers, most were either nuns, or the female relatives of male musicians – such as Francesca Caccini and Barbara Strozzi. Of earlier nun musicians, the best known is the 12th-century composer, Hildegard of Bingen. Well into the nineteenth century, women could only enter

190   Bowers, Jane and Tick, Judith, *Women Making Music: the Western Art Tradition 1150-1950* (Macmillan, 1986) p5

the profession as private music teachers, very rarely allowed into institutional teaching posts.

Concepts of gender have informed, and still do to an extent, musicological analysis. According to Marcia Citron (1993), the sonata form itself, 'one of the most important structural plans of the last 250 years',[191]was conceived in terms of a male-female dualism, which, while it may serve to illustrate the structural architectonics of the form, also reinforces ideas about the male as socially superior and the female as inferior. In this form of analysis, the first subject is strong and superior – masculine – (and related to the tonic) and the second subject is gentler, less important and incomplete, less 'perfect' – feminine. Phrases are described as having weak (ie, 'feminine') endings. This makes the 'masculine' the strong norm, from which the weak 'feminine' deviates. This is not an accidental use of language; such value-laden references to gender tell us as much about male and female social roles as they do about music.

The relationship between the high viols, their repertoire(s) and the position of women may appear to be a relatively marginal corner of musical history. However, for that very reason, it contributes to insights that question or expand concepts of the idiomatic and gender, insofar as we apply them to music and its performance today.

---

191   Citron, Marcia J., *Gender and the Musical Canon* (CUP, 1993) p132

CHAPTER SEVEN

The Early Music Revival

Authenticity, interpretation, intention

Shibboleth: catchword, esp. Old-fashioned and generally abandoned doctrine or formula of a party or sect (Heb., ear of corn).

Ploughshares: implement for cutting furrows in soil and turning it in.

(The Concise Oxford Dictionary)

In the second half of the twentieth century the insights and practices of the early music movement were subsumed into the phrase 'historically informed performance'. From marginal excavation, the principles of 'authenticity', 'interpretation' and 'intention' extended to be applied to music written before and after 1750. As Harry Haskell wrote, in his history of the early music revival:

A distinction must now be drawn between the early music revival ... and what has come to be called the historical performance movement.[192]

Conductor Roger Norrington worked since the 1960s with period-instrument orchestras, such as the Orchestra of the Age of Enlightenment, as well as symphony orchestras, with nineteenth-century (and later) repertoire. He demonstrated the breadth of

192   Haskell, Harry, *The Early Music Revival* (Thames and Hudson, 1988)

possibilities in the concept of historically informed performance:

The stunning difference between the sound of the Hanover Band and (say) Karajan's Berlin Philharmonic is enough to make us wonder if, in fact, Beethoven on original instruments is not just as much a revelation as Bach.[193]

However, even at the end of the twentieth century, there was still a way to go, as Roy Goodman pointed out in a Radio 3 broadcast:

... we haven't yet reached the day when the concept of playing in period-style all repertoires of music is part of the normal course of all undergraduate students.[194]

This comment came a decade after the February 1984 issue of *Early Music*, where editor Nicholas Kenyon generated a discussion called 'The Limits of Authenticity', where the concepts of 'authenticity', the composer's 'intentions' and the implications of 'interpretation' were explored. He continued with a collection of papers/articles from conferences at Oberlin College during 1986-7.[195]

In his book, Haskell pinpointed authenticity and intention, two of the three main principles of the early music movement:

In a sense, the history of the movement is the history of the search for authenticity – or, more accurately, the history of changing concepts of authenticity – in the performance of early music.

... to enter, through a kind of spiritual transmigration, the mind of a composer of another era – has long been the underlying premise of the historical performance movement.[196]

---

193   Norrington, Sir Roger, 'In Tune with the Time', *The Guardian* (14 March 2009), quoted in Robbins Landon, H.C., *Early Music* July 1982)
194   Quoted in 'Viewpoint', Bruce Jameson, *Early Music News* (January, 1994)
195   Kenyon, Nicholas, ed., *Authenticity and Early Music* (OUP, 1988)
196   Ibid, p175

Interpretation and Authenticity

The three initiating twentieth-century texts on music before 1750 all have the word 'interpretation' in their titles.[197] This can be understood in three ways. The first is about how to read and interpret/understand the historical music texts and treatises, which use forms of notation and signs no longer in current use. The second is how the interpretation/reading of that first category leads to the production of published editions of the music. The third is how the combination of the above two becomes the basis of what we now call historically informed performance. The first two could be said to constitute the 'hardware' of interpretation, while the third (the performance) could be said to be the 'software', summed up by a quotation from Couperin:

We write differently from what we play.[198]

The confluence of all three meaning clusters defines 'authenticity'.

✦ SHAW AND EARLY MUSIC ✦

Although Dolmetsch, Dart and Donnington's books marked different phases of the twentieth-century revival of early music (Dolmetsch called it 'old music'), the foundations had already been articulated in the musical criticism of George Bernard Shaw.[199]

A prolific playwright, Shaw was also a music and theatre critic. Between 1876 and 1950 he wrote articles and reviews about London's musical events. He was curious, spirited, informative,

---

197   Dolmetsch, Arnold, *The Interpretation of the Music of the XVII and XVIII centuries* (London, 1915). Dart, Thurston, *The Interpretation of Music* (Hutchinson, 1954.) Donington, Robert, *The Interpretation of Early Music* (Faber, 1963)

198   Quoted in Dolmetsch, Mabel, *Personal Recollections of Arnold Dolmetsch* (Ampersand Press, 1937) p53

199   Shaw, G.B., *Collected Music Criticism, 1876-1950*, ed. Dan H. Lawrence (Bodley Head, 1981)

wittily opinionated and took a keen interest in the turn-of-the-twentieth-century revival of pre-1750 instruments and repertoire.

His musical interests were wide-ranging, and it is impressive that he took such a keen interest in early music. He homed in vigorously on the issue of pitch. Modern concert pitch was not standardised at A-440 till 1939. This is now the 'norm', in relation to which early music offers historically-based choices of a) lower pitches – French baroque pitches of, say, A-415, or A-392, or b) higher Renaissance pitches of, say, A-c.460.

Shaw also pursues questions of temperament. In 1876, after attending a demonstration of equal temperament, he comments 'that acoustics should form a regular branch of musical instruction'.[200] In 1877 he observes, after a performance of the *St Matthew Passion* (without keyboard) that: 'the effect of the voices, freed from the constriction of false temperament, was particularly agreeable'.[201]

An 1859 proclamation in Paris had fixed 'French pitch' at a=435. Meanwhile, on mainland Britain, military bands had adopted a pitch of a=452, and in true imperialist fashion had exported this pitch to the colonies. In solidarity, the London Philharmonic orchestra also wanted to maintain a=452, while church organs varied between a=441-445. Meanwhile, the Americans soared even higher, Steinway adopting a pitch of a=456-458.

The King of the Belgians apparently decreed that all Belgian musicians should observe French pitch. To try and rationalise these sonic differences, in 1885 the Royal Academy of Music set up a committee on musical pitch. However, the British military announced that it would cost too much to change the pitch, since they would have to buy new instruments. British orchestras also objected, saying their instruments sounded better at the higher pitch, whereupon, according to Shaw, the committee disbanded.

---

200   Ibid, Vol 1, p71
201   Ibid, p103

Shaw has little patience with the line that the instruments sounded best at one of the modern 'high' pitches. Modern string instruments could easily tune down, he says, and he sees no problems in modifying the playing techniques of wind and brass. The clarinet is, he suggests, the only serious problem, but even here there are solutions: either the musician merely plays the A clarinet as if it were in B flat, or:

... by drawing the mouthpiece of his (sic) *instrument out of the socket, inserting washers, or modifying his reed and his blowing, he will get down at least half a tone when he is once thoroughly persuaded that no excuse will be accepted, and that the only alternatives are the sacrifice of his engagements, or the expenditure of a few hundred guineas for a new set of clarinets ...* [202]

In 1891 Shaw highlighted the consequences of such a variety of pitches. Imagine, he says:

... the Albert Hall leading off with an A at concert pitch, the church organ responding, horribly flat, with an A at church pitch, the French and German oboists following a good ten vibrations flatter, the Philharmonic men asserting the dignity of England two-thirds of a semitone sharp, and the Americans and the military coming in with a crash, sharp even to the Philharmonic ... [203]

Shaw anticipates part of the authenticist argument for music played at the pitch prevailing when the music was first performed. Apart from resulting in a better (ie, historically more authentic) sound, it would rectify the 'modernisation' of old instruments. In 1885 he remarks that:

Italian violins would be much improved by a return to thicker strings and removal of the fortifications which have been added in modern times to protect them against the strain of the high pitch.[204]

---

202   Ibid, p174
203   Ibid, Vol 2, p458
204   Ibid, Vol 1, p296

At the old pitch of Handel's tuning fork, which is a little flat to French pitch, the instrument would give us the true Stradivarius tone ... [205]

He suggests a practical way of proving the advantages of restringing instruments and reviving historic sonorities:

The Council of South Kensington (where there was an exhibition of old musical instruments) could not devise a more practically important experiment than a performance, at the old pitch, by some competent artist upon an authentic and untampered-with violin by Amati, Stradivarius or Guarnerius, followed by a repetition of the same piece at concert pitch on a modernised instrument by the same maker.[206]

... with a view to reproducing the effects heard by Bach, Handel, Haydn and Mozart, during what may be called the pre-clarinet period of orchestration. The Haydn orchestra might be revived, by altering the ordinary proportions of string to wind players, multiplying the bassoons, and, of course, lowering the pitch, which should be done by thickening the strings used. The effect of this on the tone of the basses would be remarkable.[207]

By this time Shaw was already attending Arnold Dolmetsch's concerts, seeing and hearing, at first hand, the benefits of restored instruments:

As to the viola da gamba, it is not too much to say that M. Jacobs might safely challenge any violoncellist to surpass his performance upon it. The instrument he uses dates from the XVII century; no violence has been done to it to get it up to modern concert pitch; and the tone is full and pure, and very even over the compass of the whole instrument, there being none of the differences of character from string to string which are so remarkable on the violoncello. The viola da gamba has six strings. M. Jacobs played a sonata by Tartini

205   Ibid, p320
206   Ibid, p320
207   Ibid, p323

admirably.[208]

Shaw does not have the same enthusiasm for all historic instruments:

The ... flute a bec, flauto dolce ... is a wooden flageolet the most agreeable tones of which may be compared to the cooing of an old and very melancholy piping crow.[209]

However, the potential of the old instruments displayed at the 1885 Albert Hall exhibition spurred his imagination without abandoning his sense of irony:

... the way (in the highest gallery of the Albert Hall) is through a suite of drawing rooms, furnished in the fashions of the XVI, XVII and XVIII centuries respectively, with, of course, lutes, virginals and harpsichords, according to date. The visitor can fancy himself (sic) in the very room in which Shakespeare read his sonnets to 'the dark Lady', and watched her fingers walk with gentle gait over the blessed wood of the virginals, whilst the saucy jacks leapt to kiss the tender inward of her hand. The illusion is greatly heightened by the band of the Coldstream Guards playing a selection from the Mikado outside.[210]

The fact is, we want some genuine artist to take up the work of producing fine instruments ... of giving us back the old instruments which everybody wants, with their individuality developed to the utmost.[211]

Shaw includes vocal music:

The singers, with their heads full of modern 'effect', show but a feeble sense of the accuracy of intonation and tenderness of expression required by the pure vocal harmonies of the old school.[212]

---

208   Ibid, p304
209   Ibid, p322.
210   Ibid, Vol 1, p358
211   Ibid, pp150-151
212   Ibid, Vol 3, p128

Shaw's enthusiastic evangelism changes as the years pass. Where, in 1877, he was not too concerned about a Handel oratorio given with forces of 4000, by 1913 he has a different opinion:

> ... *four thousand executants collected from all the choirs of England. The effect is horrible, and everyone declares it sublime.*[213]

🐌 ARNOLD DOLMETSCH 🐌

Arnold Dolmetsch's great achievement was to bring earlier instruments, repertoire and performance into the twentieth century. His agenda for the 'software' of performance is to revive historic musical practices:

> *Until far into the 18th century several important problems were left to the player ... Firstly, the Tempo, which frequently is not indicated in any way ... Secondly, the real Rhythm, which very often differs in practice from the written text...Thirdly, the Ornaments and Graces necessary for the adornment of the music; and Fourthly, how to fill up the Figured Basses in accompaniments ...* [214]

Reliable evidence for all this 'is to be found only in those books of instruction which the old musicians wrote about their own art'.[215] His awareness of the need for a 'translated' understanding shows how the shift from interpretation, through authenticity and into intention are important signposts:

> *In modern music the ornamentation is practically all incorporated with the text. In the Old Music the ornamentation is sometimes left out altogether, or indicated more or less completely by means of conventional signs. The composer in either case had prepared his music for the ornaments; if we do not use them we are violating his intentions just as much as if we altered his text.*
>
> *The ornamentation alters the melody, rhythm and harmony of*

---

213   Ibid, p639
214   Dolmetsch, Arnold, op. cit., vii
215   Ibid, vi

the music.[216]

Dolmetsch elaborates on the composers'. intentions, on the basis of which authentic interpretation becomes performance:

...the student should first try and prepare his (sic) mind thoroughly by understanding what the Old Masters felt about their own music, what impressions they wished to convey, and generally what was the Spirit of their Art ... how erroneous is the idea, still entertained by some, that expression is a modern thing, and that the old music requires nothing beyond mechanical precision.[217]

The strength of his convictions is shown by the use of the word 'violation', with its connotations of sexual assault – a powerful and telling metaphor. Dolmetsch extends the discussion of ornamentation to the basso continuo, and the use of the arpeggio:

Its name is derived from the Harp, on which instrument it is natural and effective to break the chords. In modern music, the chords, when broken, are nearly always broken upwards, beginning with the lowest note. In the old music many other forms were used. The player had to find out the best arrangement, and he was supposed to know how to fill up the time of each Arpeggio chord according to the style of the piece he was playing.[218]

Dolmetsch's passion and scholarship are evangelical. We must, he says:

... retake possession of its past, its heirlooms, its rightful inheritance ... by patiently working backwards, mastering each step, the now dim past of music will be brought to life, and will take its place side by side with the other arts, to which it never was inferior.[219]

We crave to hear the music itself in its original form ... Only the 18th century can be considered as conquered; a fair amount is

216   Ibid, p.88.
217   Ibid, vii
218   Ibid, p260
219   Ibid, p468

known about the 17th century although the unknown begins to make itself felt as we recede into it. But how little we know practically about the 16th century which tantalises us so cruelly! How many years will it take before we shall have revived and mastered all these unknown instruments and learned unrecorded secrets of their music?[220]

Dolmetsch was a true pioneer. He drew together information from some ninety period sources, long out of print, in a number of languages. He created ways of performing from within his own aural landscape, with no models to imitate. He was passionate about the music and its performance. His romantic desire to become at one with the composer and his/her intentions is idealistic; however, it speaks to his passion, rather than to anything which is realistically possible. His book delineates approaches to historically informed performance which still obtain today – scholarship leading to interpretation congruent with its origins – authenticity.

✺ THURSTON DART ✺

Thurston Dart is close to Dolmetsch in his crusading spirit. However, his book does not include 'early' in its title, and Dart does not define the specifics of the period to which the book applies. One might assume from the following that, like Dolmetsch, he is pursuing a similar kind of approach to authenticity. Each composition:

... is indisseverably linked with the sonorities and the styles of performance of its own time and place. If the links are snapped, the music disintegrates.[221]

The viol fantasies are usually played ridiculously fast by modern string players...Modern performers will find the works more intelligible if they bear in mind that viols need time to speak, and

220   Ibid, pp468-9
221   Dart, op. cit., p43

that Purcell's complex harmony and counterpoint needs time to breathe.[222]

However, when it comes to editing and publishing, he is firmly on the side of modernising:

To publish old music as a string of breves, semibreves and minims is wrong on two counts; first, because it gives the performer a misleading idea of the proper tempo ... and secondly, because 'void' notes ... are not as legible.[223]

... the duration of any note value has become shorter and shorter as the centuries progress ... a tendency that completely justifies the reduction of note-values used in earlier music to their modern equivalents.[224]

This also applies to performance:

Anyone who wants to play early keyboard music with insight must study the effect that contemporary systems of fingering were designed to produce; the resulting phrasing can then be expressed in terms of the fingering techniques and instruments in use today.[225]

A performance:

... must be illuminated by the fullest possible knowledge of the special points of phrasing, ornamentation and tempo that were associated with the music when it was first heard. The performer has every right to decide for himself (sic) that some of these special points are best forgotten; but he must at least be aware that they once existed, and that they were at some point considered to be an essential feature of a pleasing performance.[226]

There were – and will be – many who would argue with Dart's

---

222   Ibid, p125
223   Ibid, p22
224   Ibid, p30
225   Ibid, p132
226   Ibid, p167

wanting to have his historical cake and eat it in the present. However, Dart himself is inconsistent. As emphatic as he is about instrumental interpretation and performance, a double standard intervenes when he discusses sacred music.

When performed in concert circumstances, without the sections of the Mass, Dart asserts a definition of the 'authentic', deriving from a conviction that the music must be presented as it was originally written – in other words, unedited for performance:

> *These plainsong excerpts are usually omitted in the sources of polyphonic music ... but they will need to be restored in any performance that claims to be authentic.*[227]

The distinction here is between observing the letter of the music, as it were – each element of the original to be reproduced (notes and words), with freedom for the spirit of interpretation, according to the performer's choice. Despite Dart's respect for careful scholarship the issue of what is 'authentic' is ambiguous at best.

ROBERT DONINGTON

Donington's book demonstrates the results of extensive research and scholarship. His book[228] draws on some 168 treatises, all published before 1800, and most translated by Donington himself.

The result is a compendium of references to style, with a range of information for the performer on all aspects of performance applicable to Renaissance and Baroque music. It is still an invaluable reference text.

---

227   Ibid, p148
228   *The Interpretation of Early Music* (Faber, 1963)

✤ THE CULTURAL CONTEXT ✤

Haskell describes an onset of 'Elizabethan fever' in early twentieth-century literature and music.[229] As far as the former was concerned, the fever had already set in. Shakespearian scholarship was well under way, and enthusiasm for all things Elizabethan led to changes in English literature teaching at universities, away from a classically based, philological/grammatical approach, towards the study of fiction and poetry. In music, Richard Terry, choirmaster at Westminster Abbey from 1902-1924, did much to reclaim the music of pre-Reformation England: Byrd, Tallis, Taverner and Tye.[230]

The cultural reclamation of literature and music was influenced by Matthew Arnold, whose ideas helped to transform critical and pedagogic approaches to English literature. A 1910 Board of Education report stressed the importance of inculcating a 'cultural heritage' via the 'classics' of English literature, giving teachers of English a particular responsibility.

At Cambridge University, psychologist and linguistic philosopher, I.A. Richards, developed a way of analysing literature, called 'practical criticism'. Richards declared:

The arts are our storehouse of recorded value ... They reward the most important judgements we possess as to the values of experience ... there is ... close natural correspondence between the poet's impulses and possible impulses in his (sic) *reader.*[231]

This echoes the conviction from musicologists that the composer and the performer/listener communicate via the work of art. T.S. Eliot, as both poet and critic, contributed to the reclamation of seventeenth-century English literature, and expanded Arnold's notion of the cultural heritage into a model of

---

229   Haskell, Harry, *The Early Music Revival* (Thames and Hudson, 1988)
230   Day, Timothy, 'Sir Richard Terry and 16th-century Polyphony' (*Early Music*, May 1994)
231   Richards, I.A., *Principles of Literary Criticism* (Routledge, 1924)

the relationship between art and history:

The existing monuments form an ideal order among themselves, which is modified by the introduction of the new (the really new) work of art among them. The existing order is complete before the new work arrives; for order to persist after the supervention of novelty, the <u>whole</u> existing order must be, if ever so slightly, altered; and so the relations, proportions, values of each work of art toward the whole are readjusted; and this is conformity between the old and the new.[232]

The notion of a literary tradition, conveying this cultural heritage, was at the centre of *Scrutiny* (1932-1953), a journal founded by literary critic, F.R. Leavis, his wife Queenie, and other critics. The crises of the 1930s – the economic Depression, high unemployment and the rise of fascism – also led to the shorter-lived Marxist, *Left Review* (1934-1938).

For *Scrutiny*, the crisis of 'civilisation' could be solved by reference to an idealised Elizabethan age, as a model for 'humane' values.[233] The argument ran that culture was shared between people of all classes, literate and illiterate. This 'organic community' produced 'a human naturalness or normality',[234] and its values were to be found in the great writers of the period. There were serious flaws in this idealistic argument. Literacy was only available to a privileged minority, communities were dispersed, with large gaps between rich and poor. Values were not necessarily shared.

For the Leavises, these supposed universal/generally shared values could be taught in the twentieth century by a minority of teachers, trained in sensitive responses to the texts. These would-be egalitarian ideals were shared by writers about music in *Scrutiny*. A series of articles by Bruce Pattison claimed that:

232   Eliot, T.S., 'The Metaphysical Poets', in *Selected Essays* (Faber, 1932)
233   Leavis, Q. ., *Fiction and the Reading Public* (London, 1932)
234   Leavis, F.R., and Thomson, Denys, *Culture and Environment* (London, 1933)

... the traditional life of England ... was so much bound up with the popular music that underlay the imposing achievements of the Elizabethans and Purcell.[235]

... the currency of Elizabethan prose is stabilised in the folk speech of a community ... in the same way the fine dance tunes ... that the virginalists used were an important element in the culture that bound the whole community together.[236]

The majority lived either in small towns or on the land. Their life was a satisfying one, governed by the rhythms of the soil or devoted to the crafts mass production has killed. It was a full life and a healthy one. It drew all classes together. The apprentice, who would one day be a master, lived in the family of his master, and the servants even in a large household were members of the family too... Standards were set from above but had no difficulty in filtering down to the people ... [237]

In a series of articles in *Scrutiny* between 1936-1949, Wilfrid Mellers[238] makes approving links between the model of the Elizabethan organic community and the work of modern composers. He lauds Peter Warlock (real name Philip Heseltine) for modelling himself on an Elizabethan composer – 'virile, vigorous, diabolic, the Last Elizabethan.'[239] Mellers sees Renaissance composers as the anchors of musical culture:

With the first great European composers, Palestrina, Victoria, Allegri and Byrd, the organic forms of music were evolved through the combination of melodies in ordered polyphony; hence too, was born, logically, diatonic harmony.[240]

In the present, Mellers praises Edmund Rubbra's melodic

---

235   *Scrutiny* March 1934
236   Ibid, September 1934
237   Ibid, March 1935
238   Mellers, Wilfrid, *Music and Society* (Dobson, 1950)
239   *Scrutiny* March 1937
240   Ibid, December 1936

principles, which:

> ... *re-establish the contact with these composers (Wilbye and Byrd) that had been lost to English music since the time of Purcell, so that we see that the spiritual affinity of his music with that of the music of Tudor England is not a matter of influence at all but is the consequence of a native habit of mind.*[241]

The elision between diatonic harmony, and 'a native habit of mind' recalls Hanslick. In line with this, Mellers argues that 'sixteenth-century polyphony ... is the truest (because melodic) instigator of harmonic vitality'. If a composer such as Rubbra got it 'right', he was apparently doing so because of a continuum reaching back to the Elizabethan musical tradition. This symbiotic link between past and present, implies a trans-historical organic continuity, which combines a romantic ideal with a quasi-religious belief.

The main cultural message in *Left Review* was that the arts were to be harnessed in the cause of the working-class struggle, and the alliance against fascism. There were articles on Hanns Eisler (Brecht's collaborator), Soviet music and brass bands. There is a serious, if small, attempt to develop an aesthetic that makes sense in terms of a broad social, as well as socialist, consciousness. Writing about the way music might be linked with politics, Alan Bush makes the point (*pace* Hanslick) that:

> ... *the effect of musical performance is as much the result of the conditions under which it is performed, and the associations which these may arouse, as of the music itself* ...

> *Thus in Germany today the 'Eroica' symphony of Beethoven is often played at Nazi demonstrations and made to serve as propaganda for a movement which stands for all that the composer most detested. The heroic mood aroused by the music is associated*

---

241   Ibid, June 1939

with the slogans of National Socialism.[242]

However, unlike *Scrutiny's* appeal to an Elizabethan organic community, Bush dismisses sixteenth-century madrigals, because of the class with which they were originally associated. He is also hostile to folk song 'with its romantic associations of an idyllic, pre-capitalist era'. Clearly there are problems with this virtual dismissal of the music of past traditions – while also implying a criticism of those who believe in the Elizabethan 'golden age'.

Jack Lindsay, in *Left Review* in October 1937, shows that it is possible to show developmental links between musical forms across history, without romanticising the idea of an organic community:

Latin poetry was written for recitation. Where late Latin poetry shows signs of a new vigour, it is fusing with the popular song. The great lyric outbursts of late medieval days (such as that of the Trobadors or the Latinists of 'Carmina Burana'), in which one can find all the seminal forms of the bourgeois lyric, is bound up with the socially active relations of the song. It is the same with the Elizabethan lyric. Donne showed the way to fuse this lyric with the tones of contemporary drama, and thus created XVII-century lyric forms.[243]

Both *Scrutiny* and *Left Review* consciously responded to the political and cultural crises of their time, with different attitudes to music, each with its contradictions. For *Scrutiny* the 'fit' with the idealised organic Elizabethan community constituted a model for a healthy cultural life, as long as it excluded certain kinds of music. For *Left Review* the priority was to garner music for the working class, in some way. Even though the journal had problems coming to terms with a cultural heritage preserved by past ruling elites, it did evince an appreciation of the literature and music of the seventeenth century. This was at odds with their view that new

242   Ibid, September 1936
243   *Left Review,* October 1937

music – for the people – must make a clean break with the past.

◆❧ EARLY MUSIC AFTER WORLD WAR II ❧◆

The political and social changes after World War II had far-reaching impacts on culture. The Welfare State revolutionised access to higher education, with grants for university students, and the founding of the Arts Council subsidised new work in the arts.

It was within this climate of cultural expansion that the second wave of early music activity developed. It may seem odd to link someone like David Munrow with the student and cultural revolutions of the late 1960s, let alone with international political events in America, Vietnam and Eastern Europe. In some respects, though, it was this very internationalism and a new multi-culturalism that was part of the backdrop for early music. Munrow's interest in ethnomusicology had echoes with the 'hippy' devotion to sounds and textures from India (the Beatles *et al*), and the post-war period saw the first waves of Asian and West Indian immigration to Britain. Munrow, like Dolmetsch, combined an interest in folk (and folk instruments) with an enthusiasm for music from the Middle Ages, the Renaissance and the Baroque.

There was also resonance between theatre and early music performance. A rapid increase in theatre building programmes in the 1960s and early 1970s generated small studio theatres and touring companies. In 1968 theatre censorship came to an end: until then plays could not be performed without permission from the Lord Chamberlain. As a result of this, often with the help of Arts Council subsidy, new groups formed, flexible staging allowed for closer performer-audience relationships, challenging the fourth wall convention. An important part of these developments was a self-styled political theatre movement, which drew on earlier socialist theatre traditions, using both popular and agitprop forms, and aiming for more democratic ways of working.

Apart from the grand ceremonial and liturgical occasions of the Renaissance and the baroque, the bulk of the early music repertoire was small-scale – consort music, and here there was also something of a democratising aspect. In musical forms that predated the authority (and authoritarianism, some would say) of the orchestral conductor, the democratic sensibility was theoretically built in. Polyphony, by definition, creates all voices as of aurally equal importance. Consort music is predicated on close ensemble work, with larger scale work traditionally 'conducted' from the harpsichord.

Interestingly, although they are quite distinctive fields, there are some echoes of the *Scrutiny/Left Review* divide. While political theatre saw itself as part of the struggle for a socialist future, early music declared allegiance to the past 'golden age'. The issue they had in common was that of 'authenticity'. Political theatre was creating plays aiming to represent ordinary people's lives onstage, 'telling it like it really is' – 'authentically', while part of the early music movement resurrected the tenet of the 1830s, Ranke's 'wie es eigentlich gewesen' – as it actually was.[244]

There were dissenting voices. Michael Morrow, founder of the group Musica Reservata, blew a blast of healthy exasperation in a 1978 article in *Early Music*. Beginning with a reminder about the gap between forms of notation and conventions of performance, he went on to praise the rapidly advancing skills of instrument makers, and the revival of early choral music:

What, then, about all the first modern really authentic performances proclaimed by the record companies and so many concert handbills? Nonsense. All this means is an 'imaginative reconstruction', 1970s style, featuring a few novelties that are the performer's interpretation of the translator's idea of what some 16th-century writer was attempting – usually unsuccessfully – to describe. This is not authenticity. Authenticity can only mean the real thing;

---

244   Kenyon, op. cit., p13

and no modern performance of any music of the past can sustain such a claim, any more than a bunch of European enthusiasts, however knowledgeable and skilled, would be capable of giving an authentic performance of an Indian raga.[245]

Morrow is not merely saying that you can never reproduce the past exactly as it was (a truism); he is also suggesting more subtly that you can never simply reproduce a tradition, which carries a whole range of cultural messages – the social and spiritual/ emotional elements that make an art form belong to a particular culture at a particular time. A European may learn everything about the Indian raga, and this would combine with the European's cultural background. In terms of the strict meaning of 'authentic', this would, of course, not do. However carefully constructed, the result would be a dialogue between two cultures – past and present – a hybrid, with its own validity.

In January 1983, Robert Donington offered a more cautionary assessment of the term 'authentic':

The main battle is perhaps as good as won, at least in principle.

The establishment itself is largely with us, yet not without some reservations which could be justified. It is no use our making the tacit assumption that if it claims to be authentic it is bound to be better. The test is in the performing ... [246]

He claims that the 'principle' of authenticity is that 'original sonorities are part of the music and necessary to it, together with the original intentions of style and interpretation'. This combination creates 'total authenticity'.

The problem lies in subsuming 'intentions' into the 'interpretation' which leads to performance. As Richard Taruskin puts it, there is:

---

245   April 1978.
246   *Early Music* January 1983, p45

... the vexed matter of the composer's intentions vis-a-vis the performer's responsibilities ... We cannot know intentions, for many reasons – or rather, we cannot know we know them. Composers do not always express them. If they do express them, they may do so disingenuously. Or they may be honestly mistaken, owing to a passage of time or to a necessarily consciously experienced change of taste. If anyone doubts this, let him (sic) listen to the five recordings Stravinsky made of 'Le Sacre du Printemps', and try to decide how the composer intended it to go.[247]

The emphasis on performer decision, following scholarly evidence, has led to ongoing debates. One example has been (doubtless still is) the hornet's nest issue of dotting and inégalité in eighteenth-century French music. Dolmetsch, Dart and Donington, taking their cues from the same treatises, made different choices about how to interpret (perform) the information. Frederick Neumann wrote:

Dolmetsch found a citation in Quantz about over-dotting in very specific circumstances. By linking the quote to a misinterpreted single sentence referring to French orchestral dances, he turned what was a sporty North German – and mainly Berlin – galant, soloistic mannerism into a global law of drastic rhythmic contraction ... [248]

Dart codified the French overture style ... and declared that its rhythmic contractions are to be applied to music from Monteverdi to Beethoven ... He endorses the French overture style, the international validity of the notes inégales ... [249]

Neumann, like Dart, believed that historical evidence should be the basis for modern performances, and that there must be evidence for the use of a particular style. Where there is no evidence, then the performer must make an 'informed' decision.

Scholar and performer are, at times, at odds within one and the

247   Taruskin, Richard, 'The Pastness of the Present', in Kenyon, op. cit., pp145-146
248   *New Essays in Performance* (University of Rochester Press, 1989) p21
249   Ibid, p22

same person, and the twin definitions of 'interpretation' (technical and musical) at times operate separately and at times overlap. It is the contradiction between the two uses of 'interpretation' which cause tension in the argument. In other words, in the end, a scholar may concede that s/he has overlooked some evidence, but they are unlikely to concede that their taste as to matters of performance style (ie, how the evidence is applied) is wrong if that is the sound they like producing.

❧ INTERPRETATION – ARTICULATION ❧

The earliest surviving treatises on articulation for wind instruments list examples of tongueing which combine 'dirita' with 'riversa' strokes.[250] These are equivalent to 'double tonguing', which is largely used now for playing fast passages. However, in Renaissance treatises, variety in tonguing was the norm, irrespective of speed.

Tonguing could correspond to the consonantal equivalents of 't' 'd' 'l' for the 'dirita' stroke, and for the 'riversa' stroke, 'r' 'l' and 'k'. Dalla Casa, in 1594, comments that the 'te che' combination is not particularly pleasing to the ear and should only be used for strongly expressive effects.[251] Ganassi, however, lists it simply as one of a number of permutations, without comment.

Twentieth-century recorder playing divides into different schools of thought on the most expressive double-tonguing strokes. Anthony Rowland Jones recommends the harder 't-k'[252] while others prefer the softer options of 'd' 'r' or 'didl'. Such differences in musical taste inevitably affect which aspects of the treatises are seen as the right ('authentic') kind of historical evidence for a particular style.

Issues of articulations may be less controversial (because they

---

250   Ganassi, *Opera Intitulata Fontegara* (Venice, 1535)
251   *Il Vero Modo di diminuir con tutti le sorti di Stromenti* (Facsimile, Forni, 1980)
252   *Recorder Technique* (OUP, 1986)

apply to individual performers) than the macro-issues of rhythm, tempi and overall musical structure. Thurston Dart's call to incorporate sections of the Mass has become an increasing norm in the reconstruction of sacred music, even in concert settings. The concept of 'reconstruction' suggests craft input, unlike the almost theological 'authenticity', but the practice continues to mix the aesthetic enterprise with the authenticist.

✌ VOCAL/CHORAL MUSIC AND GENDER ✌

In the 1980s, Peter Phillips, founder and musical director of the choral group, The Tallis Scholars, undertook a two-part survey of the state of musical training and singing in the cathedrals and their schools in England.[253]

The survey ends with a discussion about the participation of girls in choirs. A small minority are in favour of the presence of girls; the rest object, mainly on the grounds of vocal quality. No-one in the survey remarks on the challenge/threat the presence of girls would represent to the long-standing Catholic tradition that only men are allowed to mediate between the Lord and the congregation, in any significant capacity, and Phillips himself makes no comment on this theological issue.

The editorial in *Early Music* in January 1980, has a pro-Catholic air:

English cathedral music has survived vicissitudes which have tested its inner artistic strength to the utmost. It is a continuous tradition, despite the volte-face of the Reformation epitomised in the career and works of William Byrd, despite the inroads of the Puritans following the Civil War, England's milder version of the Chinese Cultural Revolution, and despite the longeurs which afflicted it in the latter part of the 19th century before the present revival began.[254]

---

253   'The golden age regained' (*Early Music* January and April 1980)
254   Editorial, *Early Music* January, 1980

The 'tradition' referred to is that of Catholic worship, for which the music was composed. The editorial suggests that this musical tradition has been under attack, and it is certainly the case that the ending of proscription of Catholicism in the nineteenth century left a minority of Catholics within a largely Protestant culture. It is also the case that the work of Richard Terry and Bruno Turner showed that Catholics have been seriously involved in the early music revival. The *Early Music* editorial continues:

English cathedrals are not only magnificent buildings but are still, mostly, active musical centres recreating forms of service that retain vestiges of the earliest of national rituals.

The use of the word 'service' has religious overtones. The language then veers into the quasi-anthropological 'national rituals', suggesting – subtextually – that Catholicism is, in some way, transhistorical and a national ritual for what is, officially, a Protestant culture. The 'golden age' in the title of these articles refers to what is already a staple reference point of the Elizabethan age. Here it elides the golden age with the Catholic age, a yearning towards a religion which is still somewhat 'other', once proscribed/forbidden, and a wish for it to become dominant once more; this implies (again subtextually) an argument that reviving the golden age will also revive Catholicism, as somehow 'truer' than Protestantism.

Secular audience enthusiasm for the music generated by Catholicism is widespread. Audiences have the pleasure of turning up as ersatz courtiers/congregations to hear music from Catholic Masses. They can have their wafer and eat it, without worrying about sin, confession, impure thoughts or hell at the end of the day. This is one of the cultural paradoxes of our time.

❧ RECONSTRUCTION: 1539 ❧

When it comes to the reconstruction or revival of music from secular events, the concerns are similar to those which apply to reconstructing liturgical pieces. This has come into focus with the performance of the Italian *intermedii*, musical interludes which interspersed plays.

Interest in these has come from musicians, rather than from within the theatre, and this means they are put together as skeins of music, rather than as separated interludes. Renaissance entertainment of this kind was a different kind of hybrid from opera and present-day musicals.

The following is an account of a project which illustrates some of the exigencies of 'reconstruction', particularly in relation to words and music. It highlights the vexed relationship between meaning and performance, as well as the boundaries of interpretation, authenticity, and composer–intentions. In the analysis of the division of labour and the conditions of performance, the contextual relationship of words, music and meaning will be illuminated.

The event was the wedding celebration of Medici Duke Cosimo I of Florence to Eleonora of Toledo in 1539. It was an arranged marriage, a political alliance between the Florentine Dukedom and the Spanish rulers of Naples. It is the first Renaissance wedding for which the music has survived.[255]

The festivities went on for a number of days, beginning with a welcome motet, sung and played at the gates of the city, by singers, cornetti and tromboni. Then there was a banquet, at which a wedding motet was sung, as well as a series of tributary madrigals, pledging love and loyalty to the couple. The madrigalists were costumed to represent cities, rivers, etc, all territories controlled by Cosimo de Medici. The entertainment and political values were intertwined in the combination of words, music, and visual presentation.

---

255   *A Renaissance Entertainment* eds. Andrew C. Minor and Mitchell, Bonner (University of Missouri Press, 1968)

On yet another day, a five-act play was performed, each Act framed by madrigals (intermedii), with elaborately costumed mythological and allegorical figures, who sang of love, harmony and unity.[256] The contemporary records describe the instruments played, in some detail. The play probably lasted well over two hours, and the madrigals on their own would have lasted about forty-five minutes.

On 31 March 1990, there was a concert at St John's, Smith Square, in London, where the madrigals were performed, with instrumental pieces, by Musica Antiqua of London. In the first half the madrigals were performed in their original chronological sequence, with vocal and instrumental pieces from the same period, interspersed. These were played on rebecs, recorders, viols, lutes, flutes, cornetts and sackbuts. The second half consisted of the *intermedii*, with additional instrumental pieces.

Some instrumental pieces incorporated divisions, elaborated lines of music, in the style of the period. In terms of the spirit, this was acceptably 'authenticist' – there is sufficient evidence that this was a common practice. However, the published music, in the part-books consists of the 'plain' lines alone.

The concert was then 'bought' for broadcast on Radio 3. The producer wanted the original documented music, and the published instrumental pieces were re-recorded in the studio, without the divisions, and without the added period instrumental pieces. For the producer, this was authentic, based on the printed records alone (the hardware), without the understanding of the historical performance practice (the software).

The original published play was accompanied by a documentary account of the wedding. I was commissioned to abridge the two-and-a-half-hour play, incorporate elements from the account of the event, and include music, all of which would have to fit into the ninety minutes allotted to the broadcast. Using as much as

256   *Musiche Fatte Nelle Nozze* (Facsimile, Alamire, 1984)

possible from the *commedia* to retain some narrative continuity, I devised an interpolated 'voice-over' element, where the two main 'fictional' protagonists, Cosimo and Eleonora, narrated the commentary.

It was clear that the original musical order would not work, since there were two long motets, and the structure would have been unwieldy. As is customary in radio, the drama and music were recorded under the direction of different producers. With the agreement of the musical director of Musica Antiqua and the overall radio producer, I re-ordered the music to intersperse the newly structured drama, so that it would constitute an effective rhythmic shape for broadcast, words and music balancing each other.

Obviously, the original occasion could never be reproduced – no authenticity there. Neither the complete play, nor all the music could be included; broadcasting conventions had to be observed. What 'was' there, was all faithful to the original documentation, but rearranged and hybridised to create a modern presentation, technologically transmitted, which conveyed, as much as possible, *flavours* of the original – words and music. At one level, the music was the most 'authentic': played as written, sung in the original Italian, although the scenes/sketches from the play were acted in (inauthentic) English. However, the scenes were presented in a different order from the original, and the whole play was not included. It was far more than highlights, and it was far less than a reconstruction, and with only partial 'authenticities'.

The balance of meaning between words and music, even in this hybridised form, is vexed. These Renaissance plays were commonly satirical, sharp-edged social comment about arranged marriages, greed, possessions, power, manipulation and intrigue – with an obligatory – if ironic - happy ending. Between each Act, the musical interludes are allegorical, phantastical, imaginative – and yet they carry the moralistic warning/message that harmony and unity lie in loyalty to the ruler, and ultimately to the political order of the status quo.

The 'beauty' of the music covers its political message to citizens to obey their princes, while the drama undercuts that realpolitik message with the satirical truths. This is, in its way, extremely sophisticated – conflicting messages which co-exist in the same context. It can be seen as a way of pacifying, pleasing supporters and opposition, who can each choose the message they agree with, and like best: satirical play, or polemical music? In the case of the radio broadcast, the satirical play (plus documentary elements) was comprehensible (in English), while the madrigals (in Italian) lent the broadcast an exoticism, separating the 'worlds' of music and words.

This Italian/English divide ironically undermines the ideology of political harmony and unity which the words of the madrigals preach, and which symbolise the romantic Golden Age beloved by some early music revivalists. The message of the broadcast was that of satirical/commedia send-up, with pretty, exotic (words and music) sounds as interludes.

Conversely, when the *intermedii* are performed alone – they are conveying the madrigalian messages of political harmony and unity, and thus are also supporting what was often a despotic form of rulership. The political pills (the words) sugar-coat (the music). These messages were clearly 'intended' to be conveyed to the historic courts and audiences – however, not by the composers or performers, but by the aristocratic patrons who commissioned them.

Conclusion

This chapter has pursued two lines of argument. The first is that the ideologies which informed the early music revival in the twentieth century were linked with developments in other arts, particularly literature and the theatre. The second line of argument has been based on an interrogation of the three key concepts which have guided and defined (and sometimes confined) the development of the early music revival: interpretation, authenticity and intention.

As we saw, the concept of 'interpretation' was the initial driving force, allowing a link between the merely technical matter of discovering and reading old texts – musical and treatise – and 'interpreting' their relevance to contemporary performance practice and musical style. In the debate on dotting and inégalité we see a paradigm of this in operation.

The concept of 'authenticity' also has a technical dimension – the reconstruction of the hardware. At the other end is the issue of what (if any) relationship there might be between the performed event and its history. It is clear that there can be no model answer, since the question about what is authentic can only ever be partially answered, and only ever selectively applied. Time and history can never be rolled back. What can be argued is that there is a distinction between the letter and the spirit of authenticist approaches, and where the meanings in these approaches lie; indeed, how the meanings from past to present might (if at all) be reconfigured, or even reversed. Arguably, the concept of interpretation, which must come into play in reviving earlier repertoire, is what conspires to undermine through-going authenticity.

The concept of the composer's 'intention' is the most problematic and the most dismissable. It seems seductive, because it offers a putative hotline back into the past, linking the mind and imagination of the composer with the mind and imagination of today's performer – and thence to the audience's experience. Such individualistic transmigration may be fun as a dramatic device, imagining we live in a Florentine court and are somehow custodians of its values, but it is not an analytical tool, and it carries with it the danger of fetishising (rather than respecting) the individual composer. In its quasi-mystical Romantic illusoriness, it diverts attention away from the music, its context and its messages.

The idea of 'intentions' implies that genuine critical scrutiny is impossible, and that performance choices cannot be criticised because they are done on behalf of the original composer, rather than on behalf of our interests and interpretations today. Interestingly, it has not become as serious a bone of contention as the other two concepts, and that in itself is revealing. It should be the first category to be dismissed. Composers are vital (without them we would have no music); their lives can be explored and their music analysed, performed and experienced. Their intentions, as Richard Taruskin has so eloquently argued, are something quite else.

The exciting thing about the words 'interpretation' and 'authenticity' in the 21st century, is that they have taken on subtleties, complexities, plasticities, which enable them to become the stuff that both inspires practice and provokes debate. Thanks to scholars and performers, we know far more about pre-classical music and the worlds from which they came.

From being polemical shibboleths which led pioneers into aesthetic excavation, 'authenticity' and 'interpretation' have become the ploughshares with which scholars and performers have devised and peopled a new aural landscape.

CODA ONE

Emotion

IT MAY SEEM ODD to leave the matter of emotion until the end. In one way or another, emotion/feeling is pretty well always associated *with* music. Indeed, for many listeners, one might say that feeling alone is what makes music important. We may feel something when we *hear* music, but can we define what it is? Do we feel something when we *play* music, and, if so, can we define what it is?

The main argument through this book traces a line from Hanslick, to show that, inevitably, and incontrovertibly, meaning is contextual and associative. In effect – and in brief – this is also true of emotion, which is a category contained within the concept of 'meaning'. The conditions of specific performances, along with cultural and other associations (music at a party = 'happy', music at a funeral = 'sad') are what bring out/cause emotion to be experienced in relation to music.

The fallibility of the Doctrine of Affects, variation in historical pitch, the practice of transposition in performance, along with the insights of the early music revival, all show that there can be no intrinsic emotions to be found within the tropes of musical systems. No fixed meanings, no fixed, identifiable emotions, 'there', to be identified and/or experienced.

However, rather than being restrictive, the idea that emotion and meaning in music are associative and contextual is/should be enormously exciting. It gives each of us the means with which to think about what we – as individuals – experience/feel when we hear/play music.

For example, is what we feel dependent on when we first heard or played a particular piece of music? Is it associated with a feeling about a particular occasion, a particular person? Why do we have different tastes in music? Why do we like the sound of one instrument and/or dislike the sound of another? Even professional musicians have tastes, preferences. They may like/dislike some of the repertoire, and yet they are constrained to perform it – with what? Conviction? Emotion? Within a particular aesthetic convention?

What is music about? What is it 'doing'? What does it mean, if anything? What is the relationship between emotion and music, if anything? Does any of this matter?

These questions are only the beginning.

CODA TWO

I FOUND SOME cassette recordings of concerts in which I played at Trinity College of Music. It is far enough away in time for me to be able to say how good (I think) some of my playing was, even though I was never able to learn any more about music theory beyond some scales, and only the simpler ones of those reliably. I certainly acquired technique in articulation, and an aesthetic, which was down to Philip Thorby's teaching, and the fact that I was surrounded by the sounds of music for five years. Without knowing the 'grammar' of the modes and diatonic scales, that aesthetic was gained with some? much? difficulty, but I think, from the recordings, that there was gain.

Part of my aim in taking on the MMus was to get words to take music on board, as it were. I reviewed CDs and concerts, exploring vocabularies to try and do justice to the works and their sounds. There are conventions in the ways music and words interrelate in works of art – opera and oratorio being the most obvious. Coincidental with my musical training, I wrote two poem-libretti: *York* for two voices, set to music by Malcolm Singer (performed in St Michael le Belfry, York, 1990)[257]; he also set *The Mask of Esther* (St Albans Cathedral, 2001).[258] In both cases I wrote the words first, then handed them over to Malcolm, who set what I had written. Apart from the occasional small query to me, the division of labour was clean: he didn't want to change my text, and I didn't want to question his music.

In 1991 I was commissioned by The Drapers' Company and

---

257 Published in *Gardens of Eden Revisited* Wandor, Michelene (Five Leaves, 1999)
258 Published in *Musica Translapina* Wandor, Michelene (Arc Publications, 2005)

the Guildhall School of Music and Drama to write a piece commemorating the 400th anniversary of the Drapers' Guild. I wrote *The Masque of Draperie*, in the poetic/dramatic style of the seventeenth-century masque, with rhyming couplets and dialogue, and it was performed, with music, by second-year students, before Her Majesty, the Queen, in Drapers' Hall, in the City of London. It was a bit silly, even though I say so myself, but it can be seen on YouTube, and sharp eyes will spot a student called Ewan McGregor.

In the above cases, my work as a writer was separate from the music. While I had no aspirations (and no abilities!) to be a composer or arranger, I wanted to explore more ambitious, and, perhaps, original, ways of combining words and music for performance. To do this, I drew on the fact that (among other things) I wrote poetry and drama. I also took from my growing knowledge of Renaissance and baroque music, contextual/background researches, and my experience of playing gamba continuo in the recitatives and arias of early opera – a dramatic use and placing of music.

All that resulted in what I came to call words-and-music-fantasias. I researched and wrote a series of extended quasi-narrative poems, then chose and combined these with carefully selected period music. At times in these programmes, the pieces of music were played/sung complete. At other times I took sections/phrases which were then 'scored' to underlay the words, which I spoke in performance (much as I would do in my poetry readings), interwoven with the music (in which I also played), with my early music group, *Siena*. This was, in some respects, similar to the way in which music is 'placed' in radio/TV/films. Each seamless short programme (45 minutes-an hour) was a complicated 'script', a cut-and-paste continuum, where sometimes music and words alternated, sometimes overlapped, sometimes were separate. The pieces had a number of live performances, and the poems were later published in their own right as self-standing texts.

I worked with two singers, and they were fantastic and responsive. The instrumentalists who were part of the various programmes varied in their responses to what I was doing. One commented that he hated taking fragments – he just wanted to play complete pieces. Another commented that she found what we were doing imaginative. One can never know how members of audiences really respond (they did all applaud!). However, my programmes completely integrated words and music in a very different way from the convention where early music pieces are played, interspersed with 'readings'. Flouting convention doesn't please everyone.

I received a Millennium grant to make *Salamone Rossi Hebreo Mantovano* the first CD in the UK of the sacred and secular music by Salamone Rossi, Jewish musician in Renaissance Mantua, and contemporary of Monteverdi.[259] On the CD, the poem was spoken by John Shrapnel (*Siena* 2002).

Plain and Fancy told the life and times of sculptor and writer, Benvenuto Cellini, with music from his time (*Siena*, 2001).[260] *The Marriage of True Minds* wove seventeenth-century songs and instrumental music, in a fantasia about Shakespeare and Emilia Lanier, the so-called Dark (Jewish?) Lady of the Sonnets (*Siena*, 2003).[261] *Music of the Prophets*, was about the relationship between Oliver Cromwell and Menasseh ben Israel and the official resettlement of the Jews in England in the seventeenth century. Music was by John Hingeston, Cromwell's Master of Music (*Siena*, 2006).[262]

In keeping with the themes of this book, I should venture some speculation about the 'meaning' of these words-and-music <u>fantasias for me</u>. As far as the audiences were concerned, I have

---

259   *Writing Salamone Rossi* in Wandor, Michelene, *Musica Transalpina* (Arc Publications, 2005)

260   *Plain and Fancy*, Ibid

261   *The Marriage of True Minds* or *Have you heard the one about Shakespeare and the Dark (Jewish?) Lady of the Sonnets?* Ibid

262   *Music of the Prophets* Wandor, Michelene (Arc Publications, 2006)

little idea what they might have thought in general. A couple of people were very rude (in my hearing!), because they were not interested in the words, and were frustrated that the music was, at times, fragmented. After all, they had come to what was billed as a concert, and were not expecting (or interested in) words which were not sung. One or two people said nice things to me.

I was absorbed and enthusiastic in the hard work involved in researching, writing the words, finding the music, compiling the programmes, placing some pieces of music complete, at other times underlaying the spoken words with musical fragments. I was making something new which had not been there before. Coincidentally, when Salamone Rossi set a series of Hebrew texts to Italianate polyphony in the 17th century, they were introduced as 'something new in the land'. In no way would I compare myself to Rossi, but there is something of an echo in the air. In the case of my 'fantasias', the 'old' music framed and punctuated the 'new' words, each long narrative and evocative poem with its own messages, and the poems themselves framed the music.

In terms of emotion, this was very mixed. Great pleasure and pride in what I had created; rehearsals were sometimes exciting and rewarding, sometimes frustrating, when it was palpable that one or more musicians were disinterested, and couldn't wait to get away. There was great difficulty and frustration in trying to book performances and generate interest in the early music performance circuit. In the end I stopped bothering. I have some sadness about that, but, realistically, the early movement world is relatively small, and very few performers (brilliant as many are) make much of a living out of it. And I was earning my living as a writer anyway.

The pleasure in performance (music, drama, anything else) is when the event feels easy and effortless, the pinnacle of the hard work which has gone into its preparation. Performing to an audience also has its pleasures, displaying art and skill, receiving close attention, applause, acknowledgement. Whatever else, music is only ever, briefly pure, the emotions and meanings rarely simple.

What is music about – for you? What does it mean to you? What do you feel when you hear/play music? Does any of this matter?

I still have the soprano recorder which I was given when I was ten.

BIBLIOGRAPHY

VdGSA: Viola da Gamba Society of America
VdGSGB: Viola da Gamba Society of Great Britain

Abel, C.F., *27 Pieces for the Viola da Gamba* (Facsimile, ed. Walter Knape, Alamire, 1993)

Agren, Carl Hugo, 'Diatonic fingering on treble and pardessus viols' (*Chelys*, Vol 13, 1984)

Agren, Carl H., 'The ignoble art of deleting treble viol music' (Newsletter, VdGSGB, January 1993)

Agren, Carl Hugo, 'The use of higher positions on the treble viol' (*Chelys*, Vol 19, 1990)

Anon., *Sonata in C Major* c.1760 (ed. D.A. Beecher and B. Gillingham, Dovehouse, 1984)

Ashbee, Andrew, 'Music for the treble, bass and organ, by John Jenkins' (*Chelys*, Vol 6, 1975-6)

Bach, J.S., *Partita* (BWV 1013) (ed. Paul Zweers, Schott, 1983)

Bach, J.S., *Six Sonatas after BWV 525-530* (eds. Waltraut and Gerhard Kirchner, Bärenreiter, 1977)

Bach, J. S., *Unaccompanied Sonata for Treble Recorder* (ed. C. Dolmetsch, Universal, 1957).

Beecher, Donald, 'Aesthetics of the French solo viol repertory, 1650-1680' (*Journal*, VdGSA, Vol XXIV, 1987)

Bowers, Jane and Tick, Judith, *Women Making Music; the Western Art Tradition 1150-1950* (Macmillan, 1986)

Boyd, Malcolm and Rayson, John, 'The gentleman's diversion' (*Early Music*, 1982)

Budd, Malcolm, *Music and the Emotions* (Routledge, 1985)

Bush, Alan, *In my Eighth Decade and Other Essays* (Stanmore Press, 1980)

Caldwell, John, *Editing Early Music* (OUP, 1985)

Cannon, Beekman C., *Johann Matheson: Spectator in Music* (Yale, 1947)

Carr, E.H., *What is History?* (Pelican, 1972)

Catch, John R., 'Bach's violetta: a conjecture' (*Chelys*, Vol 21, 1992)

Catch, John R., 'The Gambino' (*Chelys*, Vol 11, 1982)

Citron, Marcia, *Gender and the Musical Canon* (University of Illinois Press, 1993)

Collingwood, R.G., *The Principles of Art* (OUP, 1937)

Cone, Edward, *Musical Form and Musical Performance* (Norton, 1968)

Cook, Nicholas, *Music, Imagination and Culture* (OUP, 1992)

Cook, Nicholas, and Everist, Mark, eds., *Rethinking Music* (OUP, 1999)

Corelli, A., *Sonata in C major, Op 5, no 3*, ed. David Lasocki (Musica Rara, 1974)

Corelli, A., *Sonata in F major, Op 5, no 4*, ed. David Lasocki (Hargail, 1977)

Corelli, A., *Sonatas for viol and basso continuo*, ed. Hazelle Miloradovitch (Facsimile, Alamire, 1989)

Corelli, A., *Sonate a Violino e Violone o Cembalo, op V*, Rome 1700 (Facsimile, SPES, Rome, 1979)

Croce, Benedetto, *Guide to Aesthetics* (Bobbs Merrill, 1985)

Culler, Jonathan, *Saussure* (Fontana, 1976)

Cyr, Mary, 'Traditions of solo viol playing in France, and the music of Morel' (*Journal*, VdGSA, Vol X, 1973)

Dalhaus, Carl, *Esthetics of Music* trans. William Austin (CUP, 1990)

Dalhaus, Carl, *Foundations of Music History* trans. J.B. Robinson (CUP, 1989)

Dart, Thurston, *The Interpretation of Music* (Hutchinson, 1954)

Dolmetsch, Arnold, *The Interpretation of the Music of the XVII and XVIII Centuries* (London, 1915)

Dolmetsch, Arnold, 'The Viols' (*The Consort*, 1904)

Dolmetsch, Mabel, *Personal Recollections of Arnold Dolmetsch* (Ampersand Press, 1957)

Dolmetsch, Natalie, *The Viola da Gamba* (Hinrichson, 1962)

Donington, Robert, *The Interpretation of Early Music* (Faber, 1990)

Dubuisson, 1666, ed. Barbara Coeyman (Dovehouse Editions, 1980)

Eagleton, Terry, *Marxism and Literary Criticism* (Methuen, 1976).

Early Music eds. J. M. Thomson, Nicholas Kenyon, Tess Knighton (OUP, 1973)

Eliot, T. S., 'The Metaphysical Poets', in *Selected Essays* (Faber, 1932)

Forqueray, le Pere, *Pièces de Viole avec la Basse Continue*, Paris, 1747 (Facsimile, Minkoff, 1976)

Ganassi dal Fontego, Sylvestro, *Regola Rubertina* 1542-43, trans. Hildemarie Peter (Robert Lienau, 1972)

Gordon, J., 'Telemann's use of the viol as a solo or concertante instrument' (*Journal*, VdGSA, Vol XVII, 1980)

Green, Barry, with Gallwey, W. Timothy *The Inner Game of Music* (Pan, 1987)

Green, Robert A., 'Charles Dolle's first work for Pardessus de viole' (*Journal*, VdGSA, Vol XVIII, 1981)

Green, Robert A., 'The pardessus de viole and its literature' (*Early Music,* July, 1982)

Green, Robert, 'The treble viol in 17th-century France and the origins of the pardessus de viole' (*Journal*, VdGSA, Vol XXIII, 1986)

Grummer, Paul, *Viola da Gamba Schule* (Anton J. Benjamin, 1928)

Hanslick, Eduard, *The Beautiful in Music* trans. Gustav Cohen (Novello, 1891)

Haskell, Harry, *The Early Music Revival* (Thames and Hudson, 1988)

Heudelinne, Louis, *Trois Suites de Pièces a Deux Violles, 1701* (Atelier Philidor, 2015)

Hickman, Roger, 'The censored publications of "The art of playing on the violin", or Geminiani unshaken' (*Early Music*, 1983)

Holman, Peter, *Four and Twenty Fiddlers: the Violin at the English Court 1540-1690* (OUP, 1993)

Holman, Peter, 'The English Royal Violin Consort in the sixteenth century' *(Proceedings of the RMA,* Vol 109, 1982-3)

Holman, Peter, 'Thomas Baltzar, the Incomparable Lubicer on the violin' *(Chelys,* Vol 13, 1984)

Hotteterre, Jacques-Martin, *Principles of the Flute, Recorder and Oboe* trans. Paul Marshall Douglas (Dover, 1983)

Hotteterre-le-Romain, *L'Art de Preluder sur la Flute Traversiere, sur la Flute a Bec, sur le Haubois, et autres instruments de Dessus, 1719* (Facsimile, Minkoff, 1978)

Johnson, Jane T., 'Violin versus viol in English fantasia-suites' *(Journal,* VdGSA, 1978)

Keller, Hans, *Criticism* (Faber, 1987)

Kenyon, Nicholas, *Authenticity and Early Music* (OUP, 1988)

Kerman, Joseph, *Contemplating Music: Challenges to Musicology* (Harvard University Press, 1985)

Kinney, Gordon J., 'Telemann's use of the viol as a solo or concertante instrument' *(Journal,* VdGSA, Vol XVII, 1980)

Leavis, F.R., and Thompson, Denys, *Culture and Environment* (Chatto & Windus, 1964)

Leavis, Q.D., *Fiction and the Reading Public* (Chatto & Windus, 1932)

Left Review (Lawrence and Wishart, 1932-1938)

Le Huray, Peter, *Authenticity in Performance* (CUP, 1990)

Leppard, Raymond, *Authenticity in Music* (Faber, 1988)

Leppert, Richard, *Music and Image* (CUP, 1993)

Leppert, Richard and McClary, Susan, eds., *Music and Society: The politics of composition, performance and reception* (CUP, 1987)

Le Sieur de Machy, *Pièces de Viole,* eds. D. Beecher and B. Gillingham (Doverhouse, 1982)

London pro Musica, ed. Bernard Thomas, Brighton

Marais, Marin, playing instructions in *Pièces de Viole* trans. Ian Gammie (Corda Music, 2008)

Marais, Marin, *Troisième Livre de Pièces de Viole*, 1711 (Facsimile, Basel, 1993)

Marc, Thomas, *Suitte de Pièces de Dessus et de Pardessus de Viole, 1724* (Minkoff, 1987)

Marshall, Sheila, 'The well-fingered viol' *(Journal*, VdGSA, Vol XIII, Dec., 1976)

Marshall, Sheila, 'Viols in schools' (*Chelys*, Vol 9, 1980)

McClary, Susan, *Feminine Endings* (University of Minnesota Press, 1991)

Mellers, Wilfrid, *François Couperin and the French Classical Tradition* (Faber, 1987)

Mellers, Wilfrid, *Music and Society* (Dobson, 1950)

Meyer, Leonard, *Emotion and Meaning in Music* (University of Chicago Press, 1956)

Miloradovitch, Hazelle, 'Eighteenth-century manuscript transcriptions for viols of music by Corelli and Marais' (*Chelys*, Vol 12, 1983)

Minor, Andrew and Mitchell, Bonner, *A Renaissance Entertainment* (University of Missouri Press, 1968)

Munrow, David, *Instruments of the Middle Ages* (OUP, 1976). Neuman, Frederick, *New Essays on Performance Practice* (University of Rochester Press, 1989)

New Grove, encyclopedia

O'Kelly, Eve, *The Recorder Today* (OUP, 1990)

Old, Patricia, 'The decline of the violin in seventeenth-century England: some observations' *(Journal*, VdGSA, Vol XVII, 1980)

Ortiz, Diego, *Tratado de Glosas, 1553* (Facsimile, SPES, 1984)

Pratt, Terry, 'The playing technique of the dessus and pardessus de viole' (*Chelys*, Vol 8, 1978-8)

Pringle, John, 'The founder of English viol making' (*Early Music*, Oct, 1978)

Quantz, Johann Joachim, *On Playing the Flute*, trans. Edward R. Reilly (Faber, 1985)

Richards, I.A., *Principles of Literary Criticism* (Routledge, 1924)

Rooley, Anthony, *Performance* (Element Books, 1990)

Rose, Adrian, 'Another collection of pieces by Charles Dolle' *(Chelys,* Vol 11, 1982)

Rose, Adrian P., 'Marc-Antoine Charpentier's Premiere lecon du Vendredy Saint – an important source of music for solo treble viol' *(Chelys,* Vol 13, 1984)

Rose, Adrian, 'Music for the dessus and pardessus de violes, published in France ca. 1650-1770' *(Journal,* VdGSA, VolXVI, 1979)

Rose, Adrian P., 'Some eighteenth-century sources of treble viol technique *(The Consort,* No 38, 1982)

Rowland-Jones, Anthony, *Recorder Technique* (OUP, 1986)

Rutledge, John, 'How did the viola da gamba sound?' *(Early Music,* January 1979)

Rutledge, John B., 'Late 19th-century viol revivals' *(Early Music,* August 1991)

Rutledge, John B., 'The fretless approach to gamba playing' *(Journal,* VdGSA, Vol XXVIII, 1991)

Sadie, Julie-Anne, 'Charpentier and the early French ensemble sonata *(Early Music,* 1979)

San Martini, Giuseppe, *X11 Sonate a Due Violini, e Violoncello, e Cembalo, se Piace, Op3* (Walsh, 1747; Facsimile King's Music, 1993)

Scrutiny, 1932-1953

Scruton, Roger, *The Aesthetic Understanding* (Carcanet, 1983)

Sessions, Roger, *The Musical Experience of Composer, Performer, Listener* (Princeton University Press, 1974)

Shaw, George Bernard, *Collected Music Criticism, 1876-1950,* three vols., ed. Dan E. Laurence (The Bodley Head, 1981)

Sicard, Michel, 'The French viol school: the repertory from 1650 to Sainte Colombe (ca 1680)' *(Journal,* VdGSA, Vol XXII, 1985)

Simpson, Christopher, *The Division-Viol, 1667* (Facsimile, Curwen, N.D.)

Solie, Ruth, ed. *Musicology and Difference* (University of California Press, 1993)

Steblin, Rita, *A History of Key Characteristics in the 18th and early 19th Centuries* (UMI Research Press, 1983)

Subotnik, Rose Rosengard, *Deconstructive Variations: Music and Reason in Western Society* (University of Minnesota Press, 1995)

Telemann, G.Ph., *Der Getreue Musik-Meister, 1728* (Facsimile, Musica Musica, n.d.)

Telemann, G.Ph., *Sechs Sonaten for zwei Blockflöten* ed. Nikolaus Delius (Schott, 1980)

Telemann, G.Ph., *Sonatina in E minor for oboe, violin and bassi continuo* ed. Klaus Hofmann (Bärenreiter, 1975)

Telemann, G.Ph., *Trio in D minor* ed. Manfred Ruetz (Schott, 1939)

Tellemann (sic), G.Ph., *Sonates pour Deux Flutes Traversiere, Deux Flutes Douces, ou Deux Violins, 1738* (Facsimile, Minkoff 1985)

Tomlinson, Gary, *Music in Renaissance Magic: Towards a Historiography of Others* (University of Chicago Press, 1993)

Van den Toorn, Pieter C., *Music, Politics and the Academy* (University of California Press, 1996)

Wandor, Michelene, *Gardens of Eden Revisited* (Five Leaves, 1999)

Wandor, Michelene, *Musica Transalpina* (Arc Publications, 2005)

Wandor, Michelene, *The Music of the Prophets* (Arc Publications, 2006)

Warner, Marina, *Alone of All Her Sex* (Weidenfeld and Nicolson, 1976)

Willetts, Pamela, 'Stephen Bing: a forgotten violinist' (*Chelys,* Vol 18, 1989)

Winternitz, Emanuel, *Musical Instruments and Their Symbolism in Western Art* (Yale University Press, 1979)

Woodfield, Ian, *The Early History of the Viol* (CUP, 1984)

Woodfield, Ian, 'The first Earl of Sandwich, a performance of William Lawes in Spain and the origins of the pardessus de viole' (*Chelys,* Vol 14, 1985)